**OTHER INDIAN EXPRESS TITLE:**

| | |
|---|---|
| Indian Express | *The Prize Stories: Best in the Indian News Business 2005-2006* |

**OTHER LOTUS TITLES**

| | |
|---|---|
| Aitzaz Ahsan | *The Indus Saga: The Making of Pakistan* |
| Alam Srinivas | *Storms in the Sea Wind: Ambani vs Ambani* |
| Amir Mir | *The True Face of Jehadis: Inside Pakistan's Terror Networks* |
| Bhawana Somaaya | *Hema Malini: The Authorized Biography* |
| Bidyut Chakrabarty | *Mahatma Gandhi: A Historical Biography* |
| Duff Hart-Davis | *Honorary Tiger: The Life of Billy Arjan Singh* |
| Frank Simoes | *Frank Unedited* |
| Frank Simoes | *Frank Simoes' Goa* |
| Joshua Key | *The Deserter's Tale* |
| Kuldip Nayar & Asif Noorani | *Tales of Two Cities* |
| L.S. Rathore | *The Regal Patriot: Maharaja Ganga Singh of Bikaner* |
| M.J. Akbar | *India: The Siege Within* |
| M.J. Akbar | *Nehru: The Making of India* |
| M.J. Akbar | *Riot after Riot* |
| M.J. Akbar | *Blood Brothers: A Family Saga* |
| Nayantara Sahgal (ed.) | *Before Freedom: Nehru's Letters to His Sister* |
| Neesha Mirchandani | *Wisdom Song: The Life of Baba Amte* |
| Rohan Gunaratna | *Inside Al Qaeda* |
| Madhu Trehan | *Prism Me a Lie: Tell Me a Truth: Tehelka as Metaphor* |
| Maj. Gen. Ian Cardozo | *Param Vir: Our Heroes in Battle* |
| Maj.Gen. Ian Cardozo | *The Sinking of INS Khukri: What Happened in 1971* |
| Maj. R.P. Singh, Kanwar Rajpal Singh | *Sawai Man Singh II of Jaipur: Life and Legend* |
| Mushirul Hasan | *India Partitioned. 2 Vols* |
| Mushirul Hasan | *John Company to the Republic* |
| Mushirul Hasan | *Knowledge, Power and Politics* |
| Rachel Dwyer | *Yash Chopra: Fifty Years of Indian Cinema* |
| Salma Ahmed | *Cutting Free: The Extraordinery Memoir of a Pakistani Woman* |
| Shrabani Basu | *Spy Princess: The Life of Noor Inayat Khan* |
| Thomas Weber | *Gandhi, Gandhism and the Gandhians* |
| V. Srinivasan | *New Age Management: Philosophy from Ancient Indian Wisdom* |
| Verghese Kurien, as told to Gouri Salvi | *I Too Had a Dream* |
| Vir Sanghvi | *Men of Steel: Indian Business Leaders in Candid Conversation* |
| Zubin Mehta | The Score of My Life |

**FORTHCOMING TITLES**

| | |
|---|---|
| Alam Srinivas & T.R. Vivek | *The IPL Story* |
| Shashi Tharoor & Shaharyar M Khan | *Cricket Diplomacy* |

# THE PRIZE STORIES

BEST IN THE INDIAN NEWS BUSINESS
2006-2007

Lotus Collection



Courtesy: *AIDS Buzz, Loksatta, Frontline, Mumbai Mirror, International Herald Tribune, The Telegraph, Rashtra Deepika, Northeast Sun, Sahara Times* and *Outlook Saptahik.*



*We thank Shailaja Bajpai, Consulting Editor,* The Indian Express *for editorial assistance. Also our thanks to Ambreen Khan, Tikli Basu, Asavari Singh, Pankaj Bhutani & Sanjay Malik of* The Indian Express *for their assistance.*

This edition published in 2009
The Lotus Collection
An imprint of
Roli Books Pvt. Ltd.
M-75, G.K. II Market, New Delhi 110 048
Phones: ++91 (011) 40682000
Fax: ++91 (011) 2921 7185
E-mail: info@rolibooks.com; Website: www.rolibooks.com
Also at
Bangalore, Chennai, Jaipur, Kolkata, Mumbai & Varanasi

*Design*: Narendra Shahi
*Photographs courtesy*: The Express Group and DIG/CNN-IBN for the story 'Netas for Sale'

ISBN: 978-81-7436-677-1

Typeset in Minion by Roli Books Pvt. Ltd. and
printed at Ana Print O Grafix Pvt. Ltd., Delhi

# CONTENTS

# FOREWORD

WHEN THE RAMNATH GOENKA FOUNDATION LAUNCHED the Ramnath Goenka Excellence in Journalism Awards in 2005, I had said that if the world's oldest democracy has the Pulitzer Prize, the world's largest democracy has to have an award that not only matches it but is also more diverse in its sweep. I had hoped that an award with the reputation as the most prestigious and the most sought-after in newsrooms across the country could become an incentive for high quality journalism in India. I am delighted that the winners of the 2006-2007 awards and their work more than vindicate that hope.

More importantly, they challenge a myth that seems to be gaining ground as the new conventional wisdom in our business – that anyone can be a journalist. Today, everybody with a camera and a cellphone is a journalist and broadband is the holy grail of this new media. User-generated content is marching ahead and there are those who believe that the media, the editors or gatekeepers are no longer necessary. All you have to do is log on to YouTube for the latest breaking story.

Our business has changed in ways that we never imagined. A person witnessing an event today will have pulled out his cellphone and recorded it even before a reporter reaches the spot. There is a deluge of news on the Internet – views, news and more commonly views as news. What is unsaid and often forgotten is that we need someone to make sense of this deluge, to ensure that the viewer or reader keeps his head above water, realises which wave is treacherous, which wave is the real one and which wave is the tsunami.

It's here that good journalists have to step in with the compass and searchlights. In the end, whatever the technology, whatever the trend, journalism must be an act of character: for never before has there been a more pressing need for the media to build public trust and credibility.

There must be a voice of authority that separates the accurate from the false, the noise from the news and is able to explain what they mean.

There is another vital element to a journalist's character and that is the courage and commitment to do those stories that don't pass the 'news you can use' test. All the prize-winning journalists who you will read in this compilation illustrate both aspects of this trust with their meticulous attention to accuracy and credibility and the commitment to stories that but for them would have never been told.

Bill Cowan, the distinguished *New York Times* reporter, considered one of the conscience-keepers of American journalism defined eloquently the role of journalists in this rapidly changing media scene when he said journalism was, 'An act built on the authority, honesty and judgement of the people. When people decide what news to buy or what news is to be watched or what magazine is to be purchased, they are making a decision about the judgement, the character and the values of the journalists who have produced that news. In many ways those values are revealed every day when we decide what we don't cover, what we cover and how we cover it.'

The winners of the second Ramnath Goenka Excellence in Journalism Awards reaffirm our faith in journalism as an act of character.

– Viveck Goenka
*Chairman, The Express Group*

# INTRODUCTION

Dr APJ Abdul Kalam

I WOULD LIKE TO SHARE WITH YOU AN EXPERIENCE WHICH I had when I was a thirteen-year-old boy in 1944. It was during the Second World War. My eldest brother was a sub-agent for some newspapers including *Swadesha Mitran* and *Dinamani*. When he went to Ceylon (Sri Lanka) for work, I had to take up his job of selling these two papers in the whole of Rameswaram. Since it was war time, I was very interested in the daily news. As soon as I used to get the newspaper packet, I would open the first copy of *Dinamani* to see how the Spitfire fighter aircraft was performing against the Luftwaffe. My interest in aeronautics germinated through the news in *Dinamani*.

In 1999, I was in Tel-Aviv. When I reached Tel-Aviv, the big news on TV was that the Hamas group had inflicted heavy damages on the Lebanese border and a number of soldiers had been killed. The next day, I didn't find this news item on the first page of the newspapers. Instead, page one carried a report on a farmer from Russia, settled in a desert zone of Israel for the last three years. He had cultivated the best of vegetables and fruits in the desert area with a very high yield. The newspaper celebrated the success of the farmer. Obviously, people look for and deserve such news, which I consider as good examples of excellence in journalism.

~

I have a suggestion for editors, correspondents and reporters. In our country, it is essential to have research wings in every newspaper for training and

President APJ Abdul Kalam
leafing through the first copy of *The Prize Stories*

developing media personnel in news reporting and event analysis. This research wing has to be linked to media research in academic institutions. It would enable our journalists to carry out original research on topics of national interest and provide solutions to medium and long-term problems. The owners of newspapers should encourage research by experienced and young reporters. This will improve the quality of content of the print media. Media practitioners must realise that continuous updating of knowledge through research is essential for all journalists. For example, before certain issues are printed in some foreign newspapers, they send it to an internal research group where the data is studied, verified and factual news is generated, and only then sent for publication.

When the issue of outsourcing to India became of critical interest, a US journalist stayed in India and studied the issue and found out that the companies engaged in Business Process Outsourcing (BPOs) were carrying out business where 90 per cent of the equipment was imported from the US and Europe. Thus, the BPO industries provided an indirect market for the hardware industries of USA and Europe. Immediately, this was reported in the Indian media in a big way. Similarly, journalist Thomas Friedman, who wanted to study India's growth in Information Technology, came to India and stayed for a month and visited Bangalore and other places. Based on his news analysis he wrote a book titled *The World is Flat*. Such is the power of research.

~

*Promoting the cause of farmers:* Often, I have seen media reports on the typical problems of farmers, particularly agricultural farmers in certain regions of the nation including Vidarbha. I believe that there has to be a team in each newspaper which understands such problems after an on-the-spot study and highlights possible long-term and short-term solutions. I would like to dwell upon two important societal aspects which I came across that the media may like to think about.

During my visit to the drought-affected area of Vidarbha on 15 June 2007, I met some farmers at Yavatmal. They reiterated that cotton farmers have not been able to realise reasonable revenue from their farming operations. The output has been low and in some cases there has been a total loss due to frequent droughts. In some cases, the farmers have been supplied with Bt cotton seeds for a better yield. However, better yield from Bt cotton can come only when there is adequate supply of water. After discussions with the farmers and specialists, I found that there is need for an overview of the cotton farming operation in the region. This should include provisions of quality input, training the farmers on improved methods of farming or cultivation, marketing of the produce and action to be taken when there is a drought. To prevent severe drought, there is a need to create a large number of water bodies for rainwater harvesting which will be useful during the period of drought. In addition, there is a need for the local textile industry to work with farmers and provide them marketing support for their produce without going through middlemen. Also, the banking system should reach every village in the Vidarbha district so that the farmers are not exploited by moneylenders. The e-Choupal system established by ITC Ltd in various areas has allowed farmers to enhance their productivity and realise better value for their products. There is also the model available in Gheri Buttar, Punjab where collaborative work among farmers, industries, research institutions and academic institutions has resulted in doubling the cotton productivity. I am of the view that relief and programme packages have to be combined with a plan of implementation and targets, and an organisational structure and accountability for implementation.

Journalists may like to study the problem in detail and suggest ways to help the state governments find lasting solutions to the satisfaction of farmers.

~

*National Emergency Service Mission:* Every day we find road accidents and many other emergencies leading to loss of life and property which is much higher than the loss due to war or terror attacks. There is a method to save over a million lives every year and prevent the associated damages which has been put into practice in Andhra Pradesh. The Emergency Management and Research System in Hyderabad deals with various types of emergencies such as road traffic, accidents, and fire-related emergencies. They have developed a system which integrates multiple agencies to provide a quick and comprehensive emergency response. The emergency process begins with a call to the toll free number 108 either from a fixed line or a mobile phone. This enables timely arrival of an ambulance equipped with emergency first-aid equipment for the patient to be taken to the nearest medical aid centre. This programme has been launched in all the 23 districts of Andhra Pradesh including in rural areas and is equipped with 380 ambulances. To date over 11,500 precious lives have been saved and the average response time realised between receiving a call and reaching a hospital has been reduced to thirty-six minutes. The facility is available to all citizens for twenty-four hours a day, seven days a week. This programme is also being launched in some other states. It should be extended to all states and union territories in the country. That will enable reception of about one million calls per day and save one million lives a year.

A partnership for the mission has to come from the government, healthcare centres, and the corporate world in both public and private sectors, police and district authorities and societal organizations. Journalists can play a very important role in realising this mission by effectively articulating all aspects to stakeholders of the programme and quantifying the benefits which can accrue to society.

Journalism is truth expressed in intelligible language for the information and education of the readers. True journalism vitalises the nation. There is no room for sensationalism in it even if in the short run it might sell. It will be sheer sacrilege. True journalism is courageous, truthful, inspiring and exalting.

– Dr APJ Abdul Kalam

*(Extracts from the speech delivered by former President Dr APJ Abdul Kalam on the occasion of the Ramnath Goenka Excellence in Journalism Awards on 16 July 2007.)*

# IS EXCELLENT JOURNALISM, BAD BUSINESS?

~

**MODERATORS**

**Rajdeep Sardesai** – CNN-IBN | **Barkha Dutt** – NDTV 24X7

**PANELISTS**

**Shobhana Bhartia** – The Hindustan Times | **N Ram** – The Hindu

**Ravi Dhariwal** – The Times of India | **Pankaj Pachauri** – NDTV India

**Shekhar Gupta** – The Indian Express

**Rajdeep Sardesai**: This is the first *Ramnath Goenka Memorial Media Debate* which we hope, will be an annual feature.

We in the media, tend to criticise everyone else. We criticise politicians, we criticise the judiciary, we criticise the legislature. But we often don't turn the gaze inwards. That's the main purpose behind the topic for the first *Ramnath Goenka Memorial Debate:* 'Is excellent journalism, bad business?' Does it make bad business sense to be doing good journalism? That's the paradox we hope to discuss and debate. Let me start by asking: what constitutes excellence?

**Shobhana Bhartia**: I think excellent journalism needs to be defined by sticking to the core values of integrity, truth and honesty. But there is a difference between relevant journalism and excellent journalism. Excellent

*(This debate was held at the Ramnath Goenka Excellence in Journalism Awards function held on 16 July 2007.)*

journalism definitely captures the core values, the soul of journalism, but who is it relevant for? Something that is excellent for you may not be excellent for somebody else.

**Barkha Dutt:** N Ram, let me ask you, 'Are news judgements determined by whether your readers or viewers care about it or, as news people, do we believe they ought to care about it?'

**N Ram:** I think this is at the heart of the pursuit of excellence in any intellectual sphere. The pursuit of quality and excellence also has to be accessible. One has to have both.

**Barkha Dutt:** Shekhar Gupta, there are papers of influence and there are papers of the mass market. Are they mutually exclusive?

**Shekhar Gupta:** I would be very happy if we were a paper of advertisements. Who said popular journalism can't be excellent journalism?

**Rajdeep Sardesai:** Is there a distinction?

**Shekhar Gupta:** No, there is no distinction. I like the *New York Times*' definition of what news or journalism is about. All the news that is fit to print. What is fit to print is determined by many factors, including the market place. I would say, don't write for your mother because your mother will always love what you write. Write for your landlord. I think popular journalism can also be excellent journalism.

**Rajdeep Sardesai:** Ravi Dhariwal, *The Times of India*, today, is a very good newspaper. Was that change forced on you by business considerations, was it the market which drove you towards that? And who runs the show – the marketing man or the Editor?

**Ravi Dhariwal:** I would say that our ethos is very straightforward, it's very market-and-reader driven. We believe we write for our readers and not for ourselves. We don't write for political leaders.

**Barkha Dutt:** When you say you write for the reader, does that mean at a morning edit meeting, you say, 'Nuclear deal ... no. The reader doesn't get it?'

**Ravi Dhariwal:** I think the reader is far more intelligent. He is able to decipher what you are writing and what you are saying. We believe in the power of suggestion. All that the reader needs are relevant stories, written with a tremendous amount of credibility.

The Panelists: (L to R) Shobhana Bhartia, N Ram and Ravi Dhariwal

**Rajdeep Sardesai:** Do you think the nuclear deal is a relevant story?

**Ravi Dhariwal:** Of course. It makes headlines in every single quality newspaper. It is a relevant story as it affects our lives as citizens.

**Barkha Dutt:** When you hear *The Times of India* described as a marketing success, do you take that as a compliment or as an underestimation of the paper?

**Ravi Dhariwal:** I think marketing starts with a good product. You can't market a product that is not good. The product has to be relevant. We believe in two great virtues – relevance and reverence. If our editors do a great job in these aspects, the paper will be successful.

**Rajdeep Sardesai:** Now, let's talk about Hindi TV news channels which have taken the notion of popular journalism to another level.

**Pankaj Pachauri:** I think the problem is in the marketer's head. He thinks good journalism in Hindi cannot be sold.

**Barkha Dutt:** Is it not true that a Hindi TV news channel will spend many more hours on a child in a borewell than an English channel? A Hindi channel will spend many more hours on Bollywood actor Rakhi Sawant and even call it 'Breaking News'. What sort of class and language assumptions are we making about the Hindi reader or viewer?

**Shobhana Bhartia:** I think it is difficult to say there are two different audiences. Even within the English audience, it is very important to define your target group and then tailor-make your product for that group. You can have a tabloid in English and you can have a more serious paper. I don't think Hindi is different from English. But when you are selling the products, you must have the target group in mind.

**Rajdeep Sardesai:** Mr Ram, which do you think is the better product: *The Times of India* which honestly says they are only interested in what the reader wants, or *The Hindu* which, at times, gives the impression that it's interested in what the political readers want to read?

**N Ram:** I hate to quote Tony Blair, but he is quoted to have said, that the media is increasingly and to a dangerous degree driven by impact. Impact is what matters, it is all that can rise above the clamour, get noticed. Impact gives the competitive edge, of course, the accuracy of the story counts, but it is secondary to impact.

**Barkha Dutt:** People say *The Hindu* is a really respectable paper but it's boring. How do you react to that?

**N Ram:** It's a free world.

**APJ Abdul Kalam:** I want to ask a question: can journalism be a partner in national development?

**Rajdeep Sardesai:** Ravi Dhariwal, can *The Times of India* help in nation-building or is it about making profits?

**Ravi Dhariwal:** We like to make a person believe he can aspire, he can do better, he can better himself. That aspiration is not limited to just the nation. We genuinely believe it is relevant to humanity, being a citizen is just a part of being a person. We would like our readers to genuinely feel they are part of a bigger cosmos.

**Rajdeep Sardesai:** That's a very interesting point. You have used a word that many believe can lead to the success of the media – aspiration.

**N Ram:** It depends on the definition of nation-building. I agree the media must play a constructive role but let us take a concrete example. You have supported nuclear weapons, but I am dead opposed to India's nuclear weaponisation. Mr Advani considers building a Ram temple a nationalist project; I think it is a highly divisive project. So it depends on what each one's worldview is. Some say democracy in Iraq the Bush-and-Blair way is good for the world. We're opposed to it.

**Barkha Dutt:** Let's turn the scrutiny back onto ourselves. Shekhar Gupta, can you pick that one moment in print or television, when you said, 'Journalism has changed forever'? That one story, that one image on television or in the pages of any newspaper, including your own, that made you think, 'Journalism has plummeted to a depth that I want to have nothing to do with, but I do because I'm part of the profession'?

**Shekhar Gupta:** I think there have been many turning points in the last couple of years that have redefined journalism. One of these was the war in Kargil. The old notion of the journalist, sitting there, sending dispatches to his paper – is gone. I figured the Ws – *What, Where, Who* and *When* had been taken away from us – broadcast news, television news, had taken it away. We were left with *Why, How* and we can now discover a new one, *What Next*?

Around the world, newspapers that have survived and prospered are the ones who have gone into this *Why, How* and *What Next* business. So the business has been completely redefined. Now, TV news channels are having trouble because news comes through SMSs and podcasts. Technology is changing our business.

**Rajdeep Sardesai:** Is that the future?

**Ravi Dhariwal:** That is part of the future. People will still want a really good editor who understands what news is. He will package news in a manner which is most relevant to people. That will never go away – despite blogs, SMSs and the Internet.

**N Ram:** In several western countries, newspaper circulation is on the decline and so are broadcast audiences. Young people are increasingly relying on the Internet. But we are in a totally different situation. We are in 'growth mode'. In India, we have got the opportunity to avoid the mistakes made by major media players abroad.

**Shobhana Bhartia:** Multi-media houses will first break the news on SMS, it will be followed up on the Internet. A channel will put the news out and the newspaper will digest it, analyse it and add value. It is not one at the cost of the other. In a multi-media environment, one should use the technology available. A newspaper has a role, one that has been redefined. In the next few years, it has to do a bit of everything. A news alert is as important to your consumer as is analysing the news.

**Rajdeep Sardesai:** Time for our audience questions.

**Ravi Shanker Prasad:** It is a simple question. How long will the TRPs (television rating points) drive you? And how long should it be allowed to drive you?

**Rajdeep Sardesai:** That is an important point. But who will bell the cat? Who will say the Emperor has no clothes?

**LK Advani:** Indian newspapers are reasonably good. Television news channels may not be. I believe the impact of television on print journalism is somewhat responsible for the dilemmas that have been voiced today.

(From L to R) Shalu Jindal, Naveen Jindal, Prithviraj Chavan, Sitaram Yechury and Ravishanker Prasad

**Barkha Dutt:** Sir, would you concede that television might have done many things wrong but it has also brought vigour and energy back into journalism, including into the print media? Have we done nothing right?

**LK Advani:** Tabloids have also brought liveliness and interest to the print world. So what? That doesn't justify having only tabloids in the country. I belong to print journalism, I've been a journalist myself. Late at night, when one sees the programmes being shown, one is surprised. The anchor seems to have been chosen because he looks like a criminal himself. I am worried most about the impact of television on print journalism. It is forcing print to be sensational. One must present news in a manner so as not to make it boring.

**Rajdeep Sardesai:** Mr Ram, isn't television competing with television rather than with print?

**N Ram:** We are not taking a moralistic position here. Television is important and reaches a much wider number of people.

**Barkha Dutt:** Sometimes I feel television becomes a convenient punching bag. I think there is good television and there is bad television. If print remains the domain of serious reporting, why is print being affected by television – why didn't print remain as serious as it was?

**Shobhana Bhartia:** Print is not working in isolation. Whatever the event, television has already primed the audiences. It has played it throughout the day. Print cannot then afford to ignore the event. Once you've taken something into people's homes, that's all they are obsessed with. Television compels us, sets the agenda. You compel us to give it more importance. What do we do?

**Sitaram Yechury:** You have discussed what excellence would mean while accepting there can be nothing value-neutral – so let us not try and chase an illusion. The yardstick of excellence is getting people's agendas back on your front pages and television channels. And then, how do you present it? When Bill Clinton came to India, all papers mused on their front pages whether he was bringing his dog or his cook, what was his menu, etc. The same day in Bangalore, five Dalits were burnt alive. That story was on page nine. Now, where would you place excellence? I would say the Dalit

(From L to R) LK Advani, P Chidambaram, Abhishek Manu Singhvi and Viveck Goenka

killings should have been on page one and Bill Clinton's dog on page nine. But it happens the other way round. Is Bill Clinton on page one good business?

**Rajdeep Sardesai:** Page three has become page one. General Pervez Musharraf comes to town and we want to know about his pets or what models think about him. Is there any way out of that or do you see this as part of being reader-friendly?

**Ravi Dhariwal:** I believe trivia and titillation can work for a day, two days but they don't work for years. Newspapers and broadcast businesses are decades old. Titillation is only the spice. But newspapers build long-term relationships. I think people are serious, they want to read about serious issues.

**Meghnad Desai:** Can somebody explain to me why the Indian media is so respectful all the time? Tony Blair called the media 'feral' because it made his life absolutely miserable. I believe the media should hound, criticise and drive politicians out of public life. They are not doing their job.

**N Ram:** Lord Desai, we have had several cases of aggressive, investigative reporting. It has been done by the Indian media with balance and a lot of credibility. We have as much investigative capability as the British press.

**Shekhar Gupta:** The audience's tastes keep changing. I am an admirer of *The Times of India*. The firm is run by some very smart people. They have their finger on the pulse of the reader. When they change, you know tastes are changing. In the last six months, the paper has become more serious. When audience tastes are changing, you have to keep the faith.

# THE JURY

For The Ramnath Goenka Excellence in Journalism Awards 2006-07, the executive jury comprised some of the most distinguished Indians drawn from various fields:

Dr Bakul H Dholakia, Adviser, Adani Group
Mr Deepak Parekh, Chairman, HDFC
Mr Fali S Nariman, Senior Advocate, Supreme Court of India
Mr Keshub Mahindra, Chairman, Mahindra & Mahindra Ltd
Dr MS Swaminathan, Chairman, National Commission for Farmers
Mr Naresh Chandra, Former Cabinet Secretary & Ambassador of India to the United States
Mr NR Narayana Murthy, Founder, Infosys Technologies Ltd
Ms Rama Bijapurkar, Marketing Consultant
Ms Shobhana Bhartia, Vice Chairperson & Editorial Director, HT Media Limited
Mr Shyam Benegal, Film Director
Mr Subir Raha, Former Chairman & Managing Director, ONGC

## RAMNATH GOENKA
# EXCELLENCE IN JOURNALISM AWARDS 2006-07 : THE WINNERS

**JOURNALIST OF THE YEAR, PRINT**
Ritu Sarin, *The Indian Express*

**JOURNALIST OF THE YEAR, BROADCAST**
Rajdeep Sardesai, CNN-IBN

**POLITICAL REPORTING, PRINT**
Manini Chatterjee, *The Telegraph*

**POLITICAL REPORTING, BROADCAST**
Rohit Khanna, CNN-IBN

**ENVIRONMENTAL REPORTING, PRINT**
Dionne Bunsha, *Frontline*

**ENVIRONMENTAL REPORTING, BROADCAST**
Bahar Dutt, CNN-IBN

**UNCOVERING INDIA INVISIBLE, PRINT**
Vivek Madhao Deshpande, *The Indian Express*

**UNCOVERING INDIA INVISIBLE, BROADCAST**
Nilanjana Bose, CNN-IBN

**BUSINESS AND ECONOMIC JOURNALISM, BROADCAST**
Hiral Sachde and Khushboo Narayan, CNBC

**REPORTING ON HIV-AIDS, PRINT**
Sadhana Mohan, *AIDS Buzz*

**REPORTING ON HIV-AIDS, REGIONAL, PRINT**
Shekhar Vasant Deshmukh, *Loksatta*

**FILMS AND TELEVISION, PRINT**
Mayank Shekhar, *Mumbai Mirror*

**FOREIGN CORRESPONDENT COVERING INDIA, PRINT**
Amelia Gentleman, *International Herald Tribune*

**SPORTS JOURNALISM, PRINT**
Shivani Naik, *The Indian Express*

**SPORTS JOURNALISM, BROADCAST**
Gautam Bhimani, ESPN

**REGIONAL AWARD, INDIAN LANGUAGE, PRINT**
Reji Joseph, *Rashtra Deepika*

**REGIONAL AWARD, INDIAN LANGUAGE, BROADCAST**
MV Nikesh Kumar, *India Vision*

**REGIONAL AWARD, HINDI, PRINT**
Bhasha Singh, *Outlook Saptahik*

**REGIONAL AWARD, HINDI, BROADCAST**
Ravish Kumar, NDTV

**REGIONAL AWARD, NORTHEAST, PRINT**
David Buhril, *North East Sun*

**REGIONAL AWARD, NORTHEAST, BROADCAST**
Kishalay Bhattacharjee, NDTV

**REGIONAL AWARD, JAMMU AND KASHMIR, PRINT**
Syed Nazakat, *Sahara Times*

**REGIONAL AWARD, JAMMU AND KASHMIR, BROADCAST**
Zaffar Iqbal, NDTV

**JOURNALISM AWARD FOR BOOKS (NON-FICTION)**
Dionne Bunsha, *Frontline*

AMELIA **GENTLEMAN**

Amelia Gentleman, 36, was a correspondent with the *International Herald Tribune*. She is now working as a freelance journalist.

**THE AWARD WINNER**
FOREIGN CORRESPONDENT COVERING INDIA, PRINT

# INVISIBLE CHILDREN OF BHAUPUR

BUREAUCRATIC INERTIA LEADS TO UNREGISTERED BIRTHS, AND LIMITED FUTURES IN BHAUPUR, UTTAR PRADESH, WHERE OFFICIALLY THE CHILDREN DO NOT EXIST.

## INVISIBLE CHILDREN OF BHAUPUR

PHYSICALLY, THEY ARE VERY OBVIOUSLY HERE – DOZENS of them running through the streets, climbing on the walls, perching on the roof of the village leader's office, swinging their feet – but to the great machine of India's bureaucracy, they are invisible.

This village, and the district of Auraiya that surrounds it in the northern Indian state of Uttar Pradesh, has a very bad record on the issue of making children a statistical reality. No babies have been formally registered here for the past ten years; the official rate of birth registration stands at zero per cent.

It is a peculiar anomaly that says much about the head-spinning intricacies of Indian bureaucracy. But it is more significant than merely an administrative oversight: a child who does not exist in the eyes of the state is likely to remain forever excluded from the expanding opportunities of a swiftly transforming India.

Without the elusive birth certificate, the children have no legal status. Beyond a lingering uncertainty about their own date of birth, they are not able to obtain a passport, apply for an official job, get food rations, inherit land or prove that they are Indian. Getting educated and securing proper medical care become more complicated.

India is not good at recording the arrival of new babies. Nationwide, about 42 per cent of births are not registered; very few babies in remote rural areas and inner-city slums are ever dignified with an official record. 'This is worrisome,' a recent government paper on the subject conceded.

'We know that an unregistered child is a vulnerable child, who will forever be condemned to live on the margins of society,' said Rima Salah, deputy executive director of UNICEF.

Administrative apathy is the prime reason why Bhaupur's officials have not registered the children's existence.

The village leader, Rajender Tewary, is full of enthusiasm for the concept of birth certificates. Lecturing a crowd of villagers during a meeting in the sandy yard outside the local school, he declared, 'They are very important for the child's future.'

He expressed only mild surprise on learning that none of the children had been issued certificates.

Jaishi Ram, the official responsible for recording births, shrugged and conceded that the state authorities had failed to send any birth certificate forms to this remote village for the past five or six years, leaving him uncertain as to which new child should be awarded one of the two remaining certificates that lie in his office.

Photocopying these forms was an option he had rejected as a possibility, since the nearest photocopier was a 110 kilometre, or 68 mile, drive away.

For a long time, the district health authorities had also failed to supply the village with an official birth registration book. Instead, Ram recorded all new arrivals on a piece of paper torn from a notebook; there are no computers in this village, which is still at the pre-typewriter stage.

Sometimes these sheets would be sent to the district authorities, but because they were submitted on unofficial paper in an incorrect format, the officials at the next level refused to process them. So, according to state records, no children have been born in the village for many years.

Even with the right forms available, the process by which each birth must be registered is Orwellian in its complexity.

'The PS needs to pass the forms to the ADO, who needs to hand them to the DPRO, who should then be handing them to the CMO, who has to file them with the CRS,' said Rajib Ghosal, a local UNICEF official who is campaigning to increase the birth registration rate, using the initials for the various levels of bureaucracy that each form has to negotiate before reaching its destination at the Civil Registration System, where a birth finally becomes a recognised statistic.

At the end of last year, a thick new blue-and-white birth registration book arrived from the district authorities; Ram keeps it locked up in his office. Six births have been entered since the start of the year. Ram is still waiting for the certificates.

Children without basic rights: The missing children of Bhaupur

The arrival of Sandeep Kumar on 4 March 2006, is marked in the book in neat blue ballpoint letters, the only entry for March. Sitting on the roof of her brick one-storey home, his mother, Niraj, who thinks she is twenty-four but is not sure of her date of birth, already has ambitions for her son, who is sleeping at her feet.

'I don't want him to be a farmer,' she said. 'I hope he becomes a government officer.'

For the moment, however, a life in the fields seems a more likely outcome. Without a birth certificate, a career in the government service is not an option – and no certificate has been issued.

Her neighbour, Upasana Shukla, twenty-four, pregnant with her first child, hopes that the bureaucratic chaos will have resolved itself by the time her child is born. She knows that it will be harder for an unregistered child to fulfil her aspirations. 'I want the child to start his life right,' she said.

The Indian government has launched occasional awareness-building campaigns to persuade people of the virtues of registering their children, which has been a legal requirement since 1969.

But it is a campaign they are not winning. Because it is quite easy to exist outside the official system – schools are still accessible, marriage is still possible – there is no obvious incentive to insist on a certificate, and for many parents this seems an arcane formality.

From the government's perspective, improving the .dismally low level of registration is a vital tool in keeping track of India's still-expanding population. Although the census conducted every ten years is independent of the birth registration system, in the intervening years, officials can only guess at how rapidly the country is growing.

An improved registration system would help planners decide where new schools should be built, where more hospitals will be needed. Demographers can monitor infant mortality rates; the police keep an eye on illegal immigration.

Without formal registration of female babies, in particular, activists fear the hidden practice of infanticide by parents unwilling to bear the costs of raising a girl. Later, a birth certificate can help the authorities clamp down on child marriages.

Uttar Pradesh, India's most populous state has one of the country's lowest levels of registration, but under pressure from the central government, officials are now working to register older children, to clear the backlog. It is a gargantuan task, probably beyond the strength of the current bureaucracy.

'The sad thing is that this matters more for the people who are already excluded. The rich understand its importance and will get the certificates. The poor usually do not push to get one, and this makes their lives harder,' Ghosal, the UNICEF official, said.

'We are trying to get the villagers to register their children so they can bring them back into the system, but for the moment no one knows about these children at the state level. It's as if they don't exist.'

BAHAR **DUTT**

Bahar Dutt, 28, is Environment Editor with CNN-IBN.

**THE AWARD WINNER**
ENVIRONMENTAL REPORTING, BROADCAST

# THE LAST DANCE OF THE SARUS

THE WETLANDS OF ETAWAH DISTRICT IN UTTAR PRADESH, A NATURAL HABITAT OF THE SARUS CRANE, BECOMES A POLITICAL ISSUE AS THE STATE GOVERNMENT DECIDES TO BUILD A STATE-OF-THE-ART AIRPORT IN THE DISTRICT OF THE CHIEF MINISTER.

CHIEF MINISTER MULAYAM SINGH YADAV IS BUILDING an airport in his village, Saifai, in Etawah, Uttar Pradesh. Etawah is the chief minister's constituency and he wants that his private jet should be able to land right there. There's only one problem. The world's tallest flying bird – the endangered Sarus crane – is also found here in large numbers, in fact, specially around the wetlands of Etawah-Mainpuri and in the surrounding agricultural fields where farmers grow paddy and water chestnut. The wetlands of Etawah are a precious habitat for the birds and nearly one-third of the world's population of the Sarus crane is found in the wetlands of these two districts.

So far human activities in the area have not been a threat to the Sarus – farmers are not bothered by the birds. Ironically, the Sarus is also the state bird of Uttar Pradesh. But the chief minister of Uttar Pradesh has other plans for the state bird and its habitat. He wants to drain the wetlands and make a state-of-the-art airport. A case has already been filed in the Supreme Court of India and in February 2006 members of the Central Empowered Committee of the Supreme Court arrived in Etawah to give the final approval for the site of the airport on the basis of their findings.

And that's when I arrived with my cameraperson from CNN-IBN. We reached a day before the Supreme Court Committee was to arrive: if there is evidence to prove that the airport would harm the Sarus cranes or their wetlands, then permission may not be granted for the construction. My cameraperson and I found that construction of the airport was going on in full swing and all evidence to prove that the airstrip was home to the Sarus crane was, gradually being destroyed. As we started rolling the camera at ground zero, the area around the airstrip was dotted with the beautiful birds. Wherever we focused the camera, there were Sarus cranes. As the birds flapped their wings, danced around trying to woo each other, the destruction of the wetlands continued on all sides despite the fact that the apex court had

Sarus: Dancing to nature's song – standing in the way of Mulayam Singh's airport

yet to give its clearance. Rows of trucks were busy filling sand in the wetlands, people with axes had been deployed all along the airstrip to shoo away the hapless birds. It was important that the birds were shooed away so there was no evidence that the cranes are found here when the Supreme Court Committee arrived the next day.

Cameraperson NS Umesh and I walked all around the airstrip. The birds were disoriented. This was their habitat and they kept making attempts to land at the contentious site. I asked the labourers at the site: have you ever seen the Sarus? Such was the fear that the chief minister's men had instilled that even though the birds were all around us, not one person was willing to admit on camera that they had seen the Sarus.

We interviewed at least twelve people and each person simply denied having ever seen the Sarus crane though birds could be seen all around. Everyone feigned ignorance. And then an admission that clinched the story. A local farmer came forward and told us: '*Kal Samajwadi Party ke log aye aur hum sabse bola ki Sarus ka naam bhi mat lena.'* (Some activists from the Samajwadi Party came yesterday and warned everyone in the village not to mention that the Sarus is found here). He was a local farmer but bold enough to speak on camera.

Hours before the members of the Central Empowered Committee were expected to arrive, the entire airstrip had been cleared of the Sarus cranes. Any evidence that the Sarus cranes were found here had been destroyed. And then the story got complicated. We were told that the chief minister was himself arriving in Etawah to convince the Supreme Court Committee of the need for the airport.

The chief minister would also address a meeting of lawyers. That was our only chance to get his side of the story: did he really order the destruction of the breeding grounds of the state bird of Uttar Pradesh just so that his jumbo jet could land in his village? Hundreds of lawyers were cheering the chief minister as he addressed them from the podium, I struggled with my camera and microphone to get closer. The only media there was from the local networks. After some pushing and shoving we made our way to the chief minister. I still had no idea where I got the strength to say this but I said it:

**Bahar Dutt:** *We have recorded on our camera people confessing that they have been employed to shoo away the Sarus cranes. Are they from your party?*

There was silence. The chief minister first looked at me in disbelief. His right hand man took out a handkerchief and wiped his brow. The body movement suggested the unease my question had caused. Finally, the chief minister lashed out:

**Mulayam Singh:** *Who has sent you? You are not from the media. Someone from above, from the Opposition has sent you?*

**Bahar Dutt:** *You are not answering my question. Are there any Sarus cranes near the airstrip, and as chief minister do you not have a responsibility to protect the Sarus which is your state bird?*

**Mulayam Singh***: Everything you have said is absolutely false. And we are doing a lot to improve the tree cover in Uttar Pradesh.*

I noticed he was dodging the question. Instead, he started quoting me figures about the number of trees planted across his state. He refused to comment on the Sarus crane.

I have quoted verbatim the conversation as it had sealed the entire story for us. Following our argument with the chief minister I headed back to the wetlands. I needed some more shots of the graceful birds – but by then all hell had broken loose. Suddenly, some cars started following us. We stopped at a distance from the airstrip to try and get some shots of the airstrip. Some local goons headed towards us, at first politely asking us for our identification card and then tried snatching our camera. There was a minor scuffle and I was worried they might snatch our tapes – we still had a six-hour drive back to Delhi. We retreated. As the sun set and we left the green fields of Etawah, the birds had once again descended on the airstrip. Perhaps to claim ownership over their land. As I headed back to file my story, I turned and cast one last glance on a pair of Sarus cranes. I just hoped this was not the last dance of the Sarus. And that the chief minister's jumbo dreams would not mean a crash landing for these beautiful birds.

POSTSCRIPT

This was an environmental investigation that ran on prime time news on CNN-IBN. Following the telecast of the story, there was a huge public outcry. Mulayam Singh Yadav sanctioned Rs 10 crore from the government to prove that he did care for the state bird of Uttar Pradesh. Two years later, when a new chief minister came to power, she scrapped the project of building the airport on the Sarus cranes' habitat.

## BHASHA **SINGH**

Bhasha Singh, 37, is a correspondent with *Outlook Saptahik*.

**THE AWARD WINNER**
REGIONAL AWARD, HINDI, PRINT

# *BALTIWALIS'* HELL

KANPUR MUNICIPAL CORPORATION FILES FALSE AFFIDAVIT IN THE SUPREME COURT, EVEN AS A NUMBER OF WOMEN CONTINUE TO WORK AS MANUAL SCAVENGERS IN THE CITY.

EACH CITY HAS ITS OWN VOCABULARY – WORDS THAT can be understood only in the context of a particular area or region. Two such words that one comes across in Kanpur are *kamai wali latrine* and *baltiwali*. While the first is used for dry toilets, the latter denotes women manual scavengers. Perhaps it is not expected of them, but *baltiwalis* are vocal and confident when it comes to talking about their plight and profession. In fact, some of them even smile in the midst of pain and anger.

Sadly and shockingly, none of the *baltiwalis* whom I met in the various areas of Kanpur were aware of the rehabilitation programmes launched by the government for manual scavengers. This, despite the fact that in Kanpur alone Rs 227.80 lakh had been allotted to the District Urban Development Agency (DUDA), as a part of a scheme started in September 2004, for rehabilitation of manual scavengers and removal of dry toilets. Out of this only Rs 76.96 lakh had been spent till December 2005. That the authorities were not inclined towards resolving the issue was evident from the fact that the municipal commissioner had submitted a false affidavit to the Supreme Court stating that there was no practice of manual scavenging in the city. But before throwing light on this issue, it's important to take a look at those slums where this hellfire was consuming several women daily.

Take the case of Sujatganj. In this predominantly Muslim locality, development has so far meant only television and Pepsi. There are no roads here and no question of laying sewage lines – after all 50 to 60 per cent of the city is devoid of sewer lines. Here I met Shanti, carrying the night soil on her head and a small broom in her hand. She put down the bucket and broom to talk to me. 'I have worked as a manual scavenger since I was a child. Everyone in my family works as manual scavenger. But I will not let my daughter take up this profession, she is studying,' she said, while chewing a paan. 'The dry toilets get me Rs 1,500; there are 30-35 homes that use it and each pay me Rs 30-40 a month. But the financial situation of these families is not too good. Very few are able to pay me the entire sum every month. Thus, more

*Baltiwalis'* collective shame

often than not, one has to go for *udhari* (loan). When they have enough, they pay me the remaining amount,' she said, adding that 'it's "dirty" work; no one wants to touch us. People avoid us.'

Rani, Kalavati, Lalti, Kesar – all work in the same locality and they have some thirty-five-odd houses between them. The rest of the families have installed seats and connected those with the sewage drain outside. Forty-five-years-old Lalti said that work has reduced over the years. 'The toilet seat works out cheaper than paying Rs 30-40 a month,' she said and rued the fact there wasn't even a single day off for her. But why are so many women working as manual scavengers? Lalti explained: 'This being a Muslim locality, *parda* is observed and no man is allowed inside the house.'

Munni, Sunita, Rajkumari, Geeta, Phoolmati, working in areas like Bakarmandi, Chamanganj, Kandhi Mohal and Gaddi Colonelganj, said that there's a drop in the number of homes that employ them. 'Nowadays, we go to only a few houses, the rest have either installed a toilet seat and connected it with the main drainage or installed a flush system,' they said. They have some twenty-odd houses each and complained that connecting the toilet seat with the sewage drain has made the work all the more difficult, with the muck flowing into the sewage line. 'We have to clean the main sewage drains. During rainy season, it is hell for us,' they said. It was the same story in places like Bansmandi, Haddi Gudam, Gwaltoli, Shishamau, Purana Shishamau, Begampura, Koparganj and Premnagar.

About 95 per cent of the localities with dry toilets are Muslim dominated. Undoubtedly, the issue is linked with the deplorable condition of a community that faces unemployment. According to the families using dry toilets, in certain areas government officials had advised them to install flush systems by paying up Rs 3,000. Under the UNDP scheme, these toilets cost Rs 5,200 with DUDA bearing 45 per cent of the cost. Considering their financial situation, it was obvious that spending Rs 3,000 was as good as impossible for these families. Strangely, the government, despite having the means, did not have the political will to amend the rule in order to help these families. Clearly, the government did not mind letting its grant lie unutilised, even

No more dirty business?

Surviving in a world of muck

though there were hundreds who needed financial help.

According to former president of Rashtriya Safai Karmachari Ayog, Panna Lal Tambe: 'The government is not serious about eradicating this social ill. In fact, it is yet to take a meaningful initiative in this direction, it prefers to sit idle instead. Despite the fact that crores worth of funding is flowing in, not a single scavenger has been provided with an alternative occupation. The tradition of manual scavenging will continue till the time these people are not rehabilitated.'

In Kanpur, there are two departments which are supposed to address the issue – the Municipal Corporation and DUDA. Unfortunately, there's no coordination between the two. DUDA complains that it gets little or no help from the corporation and it is difficult to tackle the issue on its own. However, in certain areas DUDA has replaced dry toilets with new and hygienic ones, though the numbers are not enough.

The situation at the corporation speaks volumes about its attitude. It is common knowledge that governmental departments are proficient in telling lies. This time, the list of false documents submitted by various government departments includes a false affidavit submitted by Kanpur Municipal Commissioner Arvind Singh. On 31 October 2005, Singh submitted an affidavit to the Supreme Court stating that the 'unfortunate practice of manual scavenging does not exist anymore in the areas under the municipal corporation and hence, there's no question of imposing any challan on anyone'. This despite the fact that the corporation itself had got rid of 115 dry toilets, served 164 court case notices and put some people behind bars. In March 2006, the Supreme Court refused to accept the municipal commissioner's statement and while reprimanding him instructed the state government to conduct a survey and submit a detailed report on the issue. Accordingly, DUDA ordered its officers to submit a report based on a survey conducted till 11 January. However, given the grim ground reality, one is not sure whether all this will translate into something concrete.

Amid this clamour in the governmental departments, the *baltiwalis* continue to go through their daily hell, unaware of the fact that crores are being allocated for their rehabilitation and more than 50 per cent of that amount is being spent on other activities.

IT'S A WORLD OF DIRT, MUCK, MANURE AND MESS, BUT I did not face any difficulty entering it. Initially, it was just like any other story, but soon I found myself unearthing layer after layer. In the last four years, this one story has turned me into a 'manual scavenger woman journalist'. Such is the potential of the story. For this, I am thankful to the manual scavengers who irrespective of their demeaning situation have the courage to smile. I am thankful to Wilson Bejwada who has taken it upon himself to lead the sanitation workers' struggle; to Debashish Pal who works to safeguard the human rights of jute mill workers in Kolkata; to Martin McEwan of the Dalit Shanti Kendra; to Manuja Pradeep Sarikhe and her friends at Navsarjan for helping me enter into an unknown and almost invisible India and understand the decadent caste system which is at the root of the issue.

I am grateful to the *dabbuwalis* of Bhatpara in Kolkata's 24 Parganas – Lakshminia, Hari, Mala Mehtarani, Minseri Wasfo, Basanti Harijan, Rupa – who despite being engaged in such a grim occupation could engage me in lively conversations. They shared their joys and grief with me and said that their urge to come out of this hell was akin to a volcano waiting to erupt. Shockingly, these women were carrying on their heads the most malformed version of the caste system and yet, no one was willing to acknowledge it.

To locate these female manual scavengers was not an easy task. I got to know about these women initially from Shrilata Swaminathan, the president of All India Progressive Women's Association, during an informal meeting. When she mentioned this feudal practice in Rajasthan's Jhunjhunu district, I was taken aback; I couldn't believe that such a world existed in our country. Thus began my search for these women. It was difficult to convince them to talk to me – whether in Rajasthan, Orissa, Gujarat, Bihar, Delhi, Uttar Pradesh or in West Bengal. Everywhere, the administration proved to be a stumbling block – initially declining to help me and after being pressurised grudgingly agreeing to do so, with a hushed tone rejoinder that this practice would be done away with very soon.

It was particularly difficult in West Bengal. Though it was clear that this social ill was prevalent in the state, no one was prepared to tell me the exact location where it was being practised. It was sheer coincidence that during those days I read a story in one of the Hindi newspapers stating that the Calcutta High Court had accepted a PIL pertaining to the eradication of the practice of manual scavenging in Bhatpara. Women were working as manual scavengers in that area, according to the news report. It was a big news for me, but it took time to first locate the person who had filed the PIL and then it took four to five visits to convince him to speak to me. At the first meeting itself, he impressed me. His name was Debashish Pal. Barely thirty-five-years-old, he worked in a jute mill. Vocal about the rights of mill workers, Pal had taken up the case of manual scavengers in his area as a part of his fight for human rights. At the very outset, he told me that I should not disclose the motive behind my visit, as that would alert the administration and I would miss a chance to see the real picture. He asked me to reach Bhatpara at about 5.30 a.m. the next day. Driving 20 kilometres from Kolkata, I reached Bhatpara to find Pal ready on his cycle. He refused to sit in the car with me and instead, asked me to follow him as he vigorously paddled towards a teashop at one corner of ward number 17. There were about twenty women sitting there, having tea and *pooris*. They told me that they were PVs or manual scavengers. The jovial atmosphere of the gathering belied their inhuman working conditions. When I insisted that I was serious about accompanying them, one of them said: 'You can come but be prepared, you won't be able to eat for the next couple of days.' That turned out to be so true! To watch them clean that muck was a terribly nauseating and stomach-churning experience. For the next several weeks, it was difficult for me to even look at *kadi* or yellow *dal*. But for these women, this was their daily work. They took their *balti* or buckets and *dabbu* or broom-like sickles and went from one house to another in the locality. In this area, a number of houses use the same dry toilet. A huge container is attached to this dry latrine. The women would clean the container of the fecal matter with the *dabbu* and dump it into the bucket. Once the bucket was full, they would carry it on their head and empty it into a gutter or walk a kilometre-and-half to empty it into a septic tanker. That day, the tanker did not come. 'Unusual,' they said and realising that I was unable to bear the heat and the stench they asked me to leave. They assured me that they would make some 'arrangement'.

A visit to Bhatpara Corporation convinced me that it was because of my visit that the administration had not sent the tanker. Everyone there knew where I had gone, with whom, and for what purpose. It was because of me that those women were made to suffer a little more that day. The chairman of the municipal corporation made me wait for an hour outside his office and when he was pressurised to meet me, his first reaction was: 'Are you from the Trinamool? You have been accompanying them since morning.' For him, it was an issue of political rivalry, not a socio-economic one. Worse, he tried to convince me that compared to other states the situation was much better in Bhatpara, as these women got good money. Perhaps he was right, but it was also a fact that the thirty-year-old Communist rule had not improved the situation and had instead, compelled these women to earn a living through this illegal occupation. Replacing, what in local language was called *khata paikhana,* with a flush system was definitely not a priority here and undoubtedly the feudal and casteist mindset was at work to deter the administration from effectively addressing the problem. Face to face with this predicament, the officials were extremely uncomfortable.

It was the same discomfort, apprehension and non-cooperative attitude that I came across during my interaction with the Kanpur administration.

Here, the female manual scavengers are called *baltiwalis* and dry toilets are called *kamai wali latrine.* Armed with a bucket, a small broom and a *tasla* or basin-like container, these women go out to work. Unlike those in Bhatpara, these women get only Rs 30-40 per month and with the families who engage these women being financially unstable, a number of times they do not even get the entire sum. Those using these dry toilets want to have a flush system toilet installed in their houses, but the problem is one of money.

The scheme announced by the government does not include the entire expense of installing a flush system toilet in the house and these families are not in a position to bear even the partial cost.

In Kanpur's Sujatganj, Bakarmandi, Chamanganj, Kandhi Mohal, Gaddi Colonelganj – it was the same story everywhere. In the predominantly Muslim localities, it wasn't possible to install the flush system, as the area required to install one was the space in which an entire family lived.

Just like the PVs of Bhatpara, the *baltiwalis* of Kanpur are both lively and vocal. Needless to say, none of them want their daughters to take up this profession. But ironically, options are few and far. In case they manage to escape this work till they get married, after marriage their in-laws make sure that they work as *baltiwalis* for the rest of their lives.

With her caustic humour, Shanti summed up the situation thus: 'It's not about money madam, no one else would touch this broom. Will you do this work if I offer you a lakh of rupees?' This was the most blighted face of our abominable caste system that hasn't changed despite development and progress.

It's a web of lies that administration has created and the deception is not limited to Kanpur or Uttar Pradesh but is prevalent throughout the country. When the Supreme Court asked state governments to respond to a PIL filed to eradicate the social evil of manual scavenging, most states submitted false affidavits stating that the practice was non-existent in their states. In its letter dated 31 October 2005, the Kanpur Municipal Corporation submitted a similar response. Once its lie was detected, the court ordered a detailed survey. The local administration, MLA, state government – everyone turned a blind eye to the problem. Today, as these women struggle to come out of this hellish situation, the authorities are grudgingly looking towards the problem.

Be it Kolkata or Kanpur or Patna, female manual scavengers are naturally not keen to open up to strangers. We, as a society, are responsible for the hell they are subjected to. It is this sentiment that is echoed one way or the other in their conversations. Interestingly, before I could interview them, they would interview me asking about my caste and why I wanted to do this particular story ... and it was only after they were satisfied with my response that they would open up – talking about their grief, humiliations, distress. Often, they would chew paan or tobacco prior to going to work. To begin with, they would offer me tea to test whether I would share a cup of tea with them. The test was simple but significant – a telling aspect of our caste system. Their tact, experience, and laughter – everything was important in this story.

According to figures available, more than six lakh people work as manual scavengers in independent India. Despite crores being spent, this social evil continues in our country's twenty-one states – as a question mark on our independence and development.

DAVID **BUHRIL**

David Buhril, 31, is Special Correspondent with *North East Sun*.

**THE AWARD WINNER**
REGIONAL AWARD, NORTHEAST, PRINT

## RAPE VICTIMS SPEAK OUT

IN A SHAMEFUL AND BARBARIC ACT OF UNLEASHING TERROR AMONG UNSUSPECTING POOR VILLAGERS IN MANIPUR, VALLEY-BASED MILITANT GROUPS HAVE FOUND A NEW WAY TO GET THEIR VOICES HEARD. MORE THAN TWENTY-FIVE YOUNG WOMEN HAVE BEEN RAPED BY MILITANTS, LEAVING A SCAR NOT JUST ON THEIR PSYCHES, BUT ALSO ON THE FUTURE OF A TRADITIONALLY RICH STATE.

INCIDENTS OF RAPE HAVE RISEN SHARPLY IN HMARBIEL, Tipaimukh subdivision of Churachandpur district, Manipur, where valley-based militants have unleashed a reign of terror in the face of ongoing counter insurgency military operations conducted by the Indian Army.

'We are witnessing a quadruple increase in rape cases in the villages of Tipaimukh area where victims still have no medical facilities,' Lalthansang Pulamte, assistant secretary of the Sinlung Indigenous Peoples' Human Rights Organisation (SIPHRO), told the visiting *North East Sun* team. According to the Village Authorities (VA) and the victims, the valley-based militants who belong to the United National Liberation Front (UNLF) and Kangleipak Communist Party (KCP) allegedly committed these rapes. They have been occupying and unleashing terror in the region since November 2005.

Confirming the increase in the number of rape cases reported to the VA and SIPHRO, Lalthansang Pulamte said, 'The number of rape victims has reached twenty-five. The number is expected to rise. However, a sense of fear, insecurity and shame has been restraining the victims from speaking out.'

To understand the problem there is a need to know about the ongoing counter-insurgency military operation in Manipur that has resulted in the spillover of suffering and miseries for the innocent Hmar villagers of Tipaimukh. These can be traced back to Sajik Tampak in the neighbouring Chandel district during March-April 2004 under 'Operation all Clear', conducted by the Indian Army.

There are no proper roads, no public distribution system, no medical facilities, and worse of all, no law and order. These areas have been the ancestral home of the Sinlung originated Hmar tribe. In their quest for shelter, militants started occupying and annexing the villages in these areas. They started imposing and collecting tax from the poor villagers. Meanwhile, to thwart any attack from rival organisations and the advancing Indian Army, the valley-based militants started fortifying themselves by planting landmines in the villages at all key entry and exit points.

However, contrary to their design, it was the innocent villagers who have been stepping on the landmines and getting maimed or killed. The militants have taken the law in their own hands and started enforcing their brutal brand of justice. According to Vala Hmar, 'The militants belong to UNLF and KCP. They demand everything and expect us to deliver in five minutes. If we fail, we face the brunt.' Militants used to herd all the villagers together at any time of their choice. 'While doing so, they pick and choose our teenage sisters and even young married women whom they rape,' Vala Hmar said.

The militants took the liberty of lording over the poor villagers and unleashing new chapters of terror every day. The villagers found no time to grieve or mourn the loss of lives or property, as the reign of terror was relentless.

Thus civil society has been bearing the brunt of terror unleashed by the militants. The government is also to be blamed, as it does not forsee how civil society could be affected by the expensive military operations.

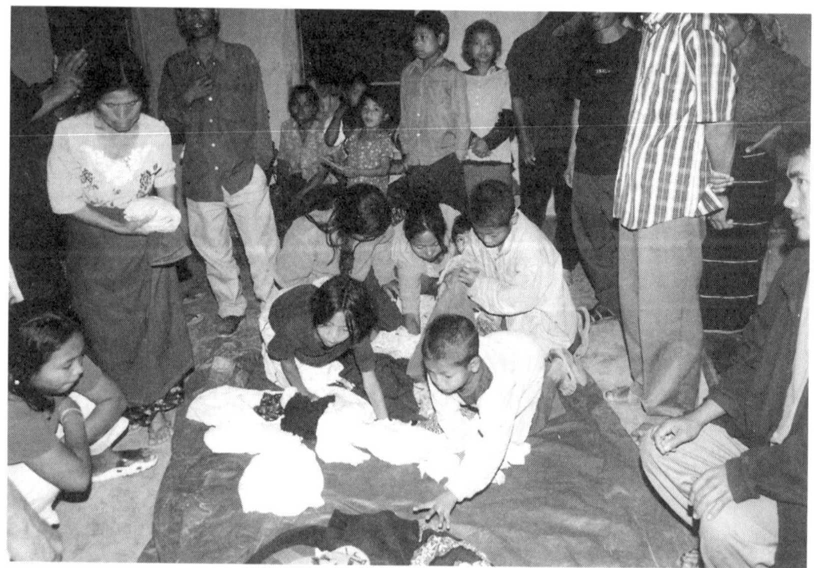

People in a refugee camp: Living in terror

In the face of the total breakdown of law and order, thousands of Hmar villagers have crossed over to the refugee camps in Mizoram as well as to different parts of Manipur and Assam.

The fear-ridden Hmar villagers from Tipaimukh have many more stories that have been hidden out of fear and shame. Village authorities have unearthed the raping of more than twenty-five innocent women, mostly teenaged girls. Seventeen-year-old Rachael said, 'I was raped continuously by three militants. I bled for two days. I am afraid I may get pregnant. Three militants also raped my younger sister who is just fifteen years old. She has not been eating and sleeping since then.' Rachael suffers from incontinence and cannot sit down because of pain, the result of the horrific rape incident on the night of 16 January.

When *The North East Sun* team visited Parbung, Hmarkhawpui and Sipuikawn, the poor villagers were busy looking out for birth control pills for the rape victims. Sinlung Indigenous Peoples Human Rights Organisation (SIPHRO) took seven of the rape victims to Aizawl for a medical check-up, as they were afraid of pregnancy. One such case turned out to be positive. Parmawi, who tested positive told the *North East Sun*, 'How can I carry the baby of those rapists? I must abort. I cannot carry layers of scars.'

Thirteen-year-old Hrietei, daughter of Zieka who was mercilessly raped by two militants is on the verge of losing her senses. The traumatised family is now contemplating migration to a far-off place. Zieka told SIPHRO, 'We are poor jhum farmers. How can we just migrate without any money? Where is the government?'

In this remote area, where armed militants reign with terror, rape is a new weapon. The total absence of law and order has given the militants unwanted liberty to act with impunity. The number of women raped is expected to increase if the victims have the courage to speak out. Lalthruoikim, another rape victim said, 'We have many stories like this. This happens all over this area, sometimes to our children. But what can be done in the absence of any security, law and order?'

Kimpui, an elderly woman in the village said, 'In small villages we are very concerned about our virtue and dignity. So, all the rape victims have been silent. There is a fear of rejection and shame too. To protect us from these consequences, we try to be silent about it. But as there is fear of pregnancy and threats of sexually transmitted diseases, the attempt to be silent has no meaning. Besides, we cannot be silent about this inhuman act. This is too much to bear in silence.'

The government of Manipur ought to immediately step in to set up counselling centres and provide necessary medical facilities for the rape victims and also for the hundreds of villagers who were severely beaten and tortured. The poor villagers are totally helpless.

Spending a few days in conflict-torn villages of Tipaimukh, the *North East Sun* team found that many of the sleepy villages were deserted. The team met many other women and learnt equally horrific stories. These young girls have no desire to stay in their villages any longer.

There was shame. There was anger. And fear of rejection too. Forty-year-old Dimnu, dressed in little more than rags with two of her kids, has already gone mad due to fear. The days and nights are spent under a reign of terror that leaves no one with any hope. Vuli, sixteen, told the *North East Sun* with overflowing tears and a whimper that she was raped by too many men to count. She was compelled to submit out of fear.

The Village Authorities, meanwhile, are busy looking for birth control pills for the rape victims. Bula, one of the members of VA said, 'There is no doctor here. But we have been looking for any medicines that can prevent pregnancy.' In a village that houses 400 to 500 families, the rape victims are more vulnerable than anyone. The families and VAs have been doing their best to cover up the incidents, but it has already become the talk of the small villages.

Any attempt at silencing rumours has not brought about the desired results. Speaking to the *North East Sun*, Thruompui said, 'I was picked out of the crowd on the night of 16 January when the militants gathered the villagers. I was taken to a house where three militants took turns to rape me. They put a cloth in my mouth. There was no way I could retaliate as they threatened to kill me.'

Zampui recalled the horrific incidents of the night and said, 'The militants came to our house to take our daughter Thrakim away. We knew what they wanted. I resisted, but was threatened. I knew my daughter would be spoilt and shattered. I tried pulling her away from them. It was like a tug of war. They pointed their guns at my head. But I did not let my daughter go. With no other option, I saluted them five times to please them. And only then did they let my daughter go.'

The stories just don't end there. Fifteen-year-old Grace, another rape victim, told the *North East Sun*, 'I was dragged out of our house. They were three of them. They all carried AK-47 rifles with them. They took me to the school building, where they all raped me continuously. I want to die.'

Zawama, a village elder said, 'Our sufferings and miseries cannot be compared to anything. We realise that our innocent daughters have been raped, but we don't have the courage to speak up. They are mourning and grieving all the time. What can we do?'

Meanwhile, SIPHRO secretary Lalremlien Neatham said, 'Things have gone beyond the limit. We are moving NHRC as well as National Commission for Women. But the people in distress need immediate and urgent help.'

In the present circumstances though, the fear-ridden villagers have little to expect from the authorities. Law and order is still a far cry for these people in remote areas. *North East Sun d*iscovered how systematic rape was used as a tool to destabilise the population and destroy community and family bonds; of how rape was used to humiliate and demoralise families and communities. However, in the face of all these untold miseries and atrocities, the government of Manipur continues to be a mute spectator.

MY JOURNALISTIC PRIORITY HAS ALWAYS BEEN TO IDENTIFY issues that have been ignored or become journalistic orphans. My prize-winning story, 'Rape Victims Speak Out', was one of them. This was an instance when the other three estates failed to be proactive on a serious issue concerning deprived and distressed people. Journalism, as the fourth estate, responded by giving these victims a voice.

I realised that this voice, was a way to empower them. The assignment for the *North East Sun* took me deep inside the deserted mountain villages of Tipaimukh subdivision in Manipur's Churachandpur district. I was assigned to look into three issues that were 'trapped' inside the cornered villages – displacement, landmines and mass rape.

It was on 6 February 2006 that photographer Naresh Suri and I reached the fear-ridden villages in Tipaimukh. To reach this part of Manipur, we travelled from Mizoram's Aizawl as accessibility from Churachandpur was out of the question. National Highway 150 was in shambles as it has not been maintained for more than twenty years. There were no bridges over the rivers either. We were lucky to be able to cross the rivers as it did not rain to flood them. Otherwise, it would have been impossible for us reach these villages.

We were accompanied by the leaders of the Hmar Students' Association (HSA) and Sinlung Indigenous Peoples Human Rights Organization (SIPHRO). I was the first journalist to reach the villages after the military operations that saw the army recapture the militant's stronghold in Parbung and its adjacent villages after a shoot-out in which one officer lost his life.

Many grey huts stood empty as villagers had deserted their homes to seek refuge in Mizoram. The vast forest covered by various species of bamboo was already in flower. The houses in the villages were pale and the forest was yellow. The villagers who were left behind bled with anger, shame and helplessness. There were no signs of immediate help. Meanwhile, the issue of the displaced people was a burning concern in Mizoram and the government and the media are still to come to terms with the issue.

The political resolve shown in tackling the crisis in the cut-off mountain villages strongly reflects the neglect and marginalisation the people live with. There was a large void left unattended by the state in the subdivision. The civil administration had failed. There was no police station. No market. No health centres. No doctors, nurses or pharmacy. There were few links with the outside world.

In Parbung village, we met an officer-in-charge (OC) from the Manipur police who reached the village on 1 February to take stock of the situation. He had no other assistance. He acknowledged the sub-human treatment meted out to the villagers as well as the rape and molestation of young girls and women. We had a meeting with the Parbung Village Authority (VA). They provided us detailed information about the plight of the people. The OC expressed his concern as the villagers did not register any First Information Report (FIR). However, it was impossible for the villagers to do so in the absence of any police station within the subdivision. Moreover, for the illiterate villagers the idea of an FIR was out of the question. At the same time the government of Manipur was far from responding to the crisis situation. The villagers were left to fend for themselves.

With the assistance of the VA, we met the rape and molested victims from Parbung and Lungthulien villages. The VA had informed the parents of the victims that we would be meeting them and their daughters. The first of the ravaged families that we met was the village pastor's. His only teenage daughter was raped. We met the pastor and his wife in their dimly-lit kitchen that was filled with smoke. The pastor told me of the 'dark and heavy misery' they were living with. He told me that he was also severely beaten up by the militants for which he went to Silchar in Assam for medical treatment. He showed us his black and blue bruises and his medical papers. He told us that he was getting better but his daughter was 'disturbed and shattered'. He said that their only hope was God and that they were praying to him.

The pastor's daughter was waiting for us in the other room. The VA, the photographer and I went inside to find her reading the Bible. Seeing us she started to weep. After some time she told us how she was raped that fateful night. With permission from her and her parents we photographed her. We left them for another family – where two sisters had been raped. The parents were sitting by the fireside. The father told us that they have been living in shame. He cried profusely and recalled his helplessness when armed militants forcibly took away his two teenage daughters and raped them. The mother told us that one of their daughters was still bleeding. We were told about the many physical problems their daughters had and their helplessness as they could not take them for medical treatment. The parents revealed their desire to move out of the village to escape the shame, as the entire village knew about the tragedy. The father said that it was intolerable to see his daughters lose the desire to live. After recording their accounts we were allowed to meet the victims. I went inside a room where the two sisters were sitting, heads bowed in anguish. I introduced myself and started to ask them questions. It was difficult putting questions to them – I was afraid they might take it as contempt. I was also afraid I might add to their trauma. I was fortunate they were willing to speak at all. One of them told me, 'What more do we have to lose?'

We met some other victims and recorded their accounts. We photographed many of them with their permission as well as that of their parents. Some of them were not in a fit mental state to even speak. Others had left for the refugee camp in Mizoram.

Many of the rape victims were in dire need of medical attention. While some of them complained of continuous bleeding, others were afraid of becoming pregnant. Some were severely depressed. Many of the victims wanted to leave the village to escape the shame and humiliation, as their situation had become public knowledge in those small villages.

One morning the VA and the parents of the victims came to see me. They requested me to take their daughters to Aizawl in Mizoram for medical check-up. It was a difficult situation as there was no transport facility and I was short on resources to take all the victims to Aizawl. Cornered by the situation in that fringe village, I asked myself if it was my duty, as a journalist, to take the traumatised girls for medical investigation. I told myself that journalism is not just about interviewing people and writing about them or photographing them. So I agreed to their request. I held a consultation with the HSA and SIPHRO leaders to share the responsibility. We arrived at an agreement: it would be impossible for us to take all the victims. So I asked if I could take only those girls who suspected they were pregnant. The parents agreed. There was not even a jeep in the village so we made a telephone call to the nearest village in Mizoram and hired a jeep. We had to wait a day for the jeep to reach us.

On 10 February 2006 we left Tipaimukh with seven of the victims for Aizawl.

When we reached Aizawl, the girls immediately received medical attention. After the examinations, one of the girls tested positive in the pregnancy test. At her request and that of her parents, she underwent an abortion. On 14 February I had a meeting with journalists in Aizawl. I intimated them about the serious issues that were mildly treated and under-reported in the media. I also reminded them about the need for the media to go back to the masses.

After returning to Delhi, I filed my reports. The stories became a matter of grave concern to everyone. The issue was immediately raised in the Manipur Assembly after which the Cabinet instituted the Rajkhowa Commission to investigate the rape and molestation cases in Tipaimukh. The commission held its hearing in the two villages from 18-26 April 2006 – twenty-five rape and molestation victims testified before the commission. The chief minister of Manipur was compelled to visit the villages. The CM had to take a helicopter to reach these villages. The governor of Manipur and a band of ministers and MLAs also visited these villages. The deputy commissioner, subdivisional officer, the subdivisional police officer and other district authorities also visited the villages, but long after we had. Tipaimukh and its villagers who were displaced, maimed and killed by landmines, and its daughters raped and molested, were now news.

The story shook and aroused civil society too. Various students' organisations held a rally at New Delhi's Jantar Mantar, Parliament Street, to protest the rape, displacement of people and planting of landmines. Various women's organisations also organised a protest rally in Manipur's Churachandpur district and NC Hills in Assam. Many students' organisations, human rights organisations as well as NGOs visited the affected villages in Tipaimukh.

The National Commission for Women (NCW) in Delhi, headed by its member Malini Bhattacharya, also visited Parbung, Lungthulien. Twenty-one rape and molestation victims testified before the independent inquiry of the NCW. The Naga Peoples' Movement for Human Rights (NPMHR) also visited the affected villages and met assault victims and later on they also came out with their independent report.

On the other hand, the perpetrators, in a press release, countered my story and termed it as 'concocted' and 'cooked up'. I was also dubbed as an agent of the 'occupational forces', which is the Indian Army. That is untrue. My stories on rape, displacement and landmines were not 'concocted' or 'cooked up'; they represented the truth of the untold lives of unrepresented and suppressed people.

I was happy to see the government of Manipur finally waking up and adopting measures to resettle the displaced villagers of Tipaimukh. However, the measures were insufficient if not inefficient. The government promised compensation and artificial limbs for the landmine victims. Many of the victims are without artificial limbs. Even the promised compensation failed to reach many of the family members of the landmine victims. As for the victims of rape and molestation, there have been no relief and rehabilitation measures, despite the many promises.

The Hmar Women's Association (HWA), that is spearheading the cause of the raped and molested victims, decided to boycott the 2007 Manipur Assembly election in Churachandpur district if the victimised girls and women were not provided with any relief and aid. The chief minister of Manipur requested the HWA not to boycott the election and promised to give Rs 1 lakh each to all the rape and molested victims as an interim measure.

However, till today, the government has not fulfilled its promise. The HWA is made to run from pillar to post, chasing the shadows behind the promises. Besides, two years after the Rajkhowa Commission was instituted, it is still to make its report public. In between, the commission cross-examined the rape and molested victims twice.

Throughout the period I realised the importance of the much talked about 'freedom of expression', which is the strength of journalism. I also realised that only truth has the courage and the strength to last. Journalism is not merely about reporting and meeting deadlines. It is more about reaching the unreached and giving a voice to the voiceless. That goes a long way towards empowering them.

When I was intimated about winning the Ramnath Goenka Excellence in Journalism Award, I asked myself what it would mean to those people who have suffered such great losses. I realised that the prestigious award is a powerful acknowledgement, that it encourages me as well as the victims to overcome their anguish and the loss. In October 2007 and April 2008 I met the rape victims and their parents again. They told me, 'You are our strength'.

DIONNE **BUNSHA**

Dionne Bunsha, 35, is Senior Assistant Editor, *Frontline*. She is also the recipient of the Ramnath Goenka Excellence in Journalism Award for Books (non-fiction) for her book on the Gujarat riots, *Scarred in Gujarat*.

**THE AWARD WINNER**

ENVIRONMENTAL REPORTING, PRINT & AWARD FOR BOOKS (NON-FICTION)

# A KINGDOM TOO SMALL

LIONS IN GIR LOOK FOR NEW TERRITORIES AS THE SANCTUARY IS NOT LARGE ENOUGH FOR THEM.

A LION PROWLING ON THE BEACH? YES, SMALL GROUPS OF THE world's last surviving Asiatic lions have moved out of the Gir sanctuary in Gujarat's Saurashtra region towards the coastal forests of Diu. They have not disturbed any sunbathers so far. Nor have they attacked people in the coastal villages. The Gir Protected Area (GPA) is simply too small to hold the 327 Asiatic lions in the wild, so the younger ones have moved out in search of new territory – as far as Diu, around 80 kilometres away.

'It may seem unusual to find a lion on the coast, but this is not the first time that they have reached the shore,' said Bharat Pathak, conservator of forest (wildlife), Junagadh. Lions were spotted in the coastal areas in the early 1900s, according to the *Junagadh Gazetteer*. Now, as the lion population is larger and open grasslands are shrinking, the animals are dispersing as if to reclaim the 2,560 sq km they inhabited until 1956. The GPA is only 1,421 sq km of dry, deciduous forest, a little more than half the original size of the forest. There are fights for territory between lions. The weaker ones step out. There are now three or four lion populations outside the protected area. A pride of thirteen lions live in the Girnar hills, twenty roam the coastal areas, there are sixteen in the Hipavadli-Savarkundla region and seven in other places.

The number of lions has exceeded the sanctuary's estimated carrying capacity, according to Dr Ravi Chellam, an expert on the Asiatic lions in Gir. Chellam's survey, conducted while he was with the Wildlife Institute of India (WII), recommended that the lions be shifted to Kuno, a forest in northern Madhya Pradesh, more than 1,000 kilometres away.

'Just because their population has increased in the last two decades does not mean that the long-term future of wild Asiatic lions is secure,' says Chellam's report for the WII. 'If restricted to a single site which is relatively small in size, the lions face many extinction threats – genetic and environmental. Catastrophes like an epidemic could result in the extinction of an endangered species.' The WII report points out how a canine distemper epidemic in the early 1990s at the Serengeti National Park in Tanzania affected 75 per cent of the lions and killed 30 per cent, even though there was a large lion population spread over a vast area. 'If a similar epidemic were to affect the lions in Gir, it would be very difficult to save them from extinction, given the much smaller area and relatively smaller lion population,' says the report.

The WII suggested 'preparing' 400 sq km of the 3,700 sq km Kuno forest for the Asiatic lions. The central government has accepted the recommendation. 'Preparing' this area for the lions means moving out villagers who live there and building up a 'prey base' for the big cats to feed on. The government has decided that around 7,400 people in nineteen villages will have to be moved out to make way for the eight or so adult lions and their young, who will be brought here once the prey base is adequate. Several villages have been relocated outside the forest.

However, the Gujarat government is reluctant to move any of the lions out of the state. It wants the lions to remain uniquely 'Gujarati'. 'Rather than moving the lions so far away from Gir, we are planning to shift some lions to Barda, a sanctuary near Porbandar,' said Pathak. Gujarat's Conservator of Forest (Wildlife) Pradeep Khanna said that an alternative location for the lions is not a good idea. 'We are facilitating the expansion of the lion's home zone. There is no need to relocate them. Re-introduction of a carnivore in a

POPULATION OF THE ASIATIC LION IN THE GIR FORESTS

| Year | Authority | No. of Animals |
|---|---|---|
| 1968 | Forest Department, Gujarat | 177 |
| 1974 | Forest Department, Gujarat | 180 |
| 1979 | Forest Department, Gujarat | 205 |
| 1984 | Forest Department, Gujarat | 239 |
| 1990 | Forest Department, Gujarat | 284 |
| 1995 | Forest Department, Gujarat | 304 |
| 2000 | Forest Department, Gujarat | 327 |

*To understand population dynamics, the composition of each was recorded in censuses because a pride can be taken as a basic structural unit for management. Male: Female: Cub: ratio estimated in the last censuses is as under:*

| Year | Male | Female | Cub |
|---|---|---|---|
| 1979 | 76 | 100 | 85 |
| 1985 | 88 | 100 | 64 |
| 1990 | 82 | 100 | 67 |
| 1995 | 94 | 100 | 71 |
| 2001 | 101 (20) | 114 (12) | 55 |

new environment is not so easy. An earlier effort had failed. Moreover, there are tigers in the Kuno forest. When natural dispersal of lions is taking place around Gir, why interfere with nature?' he said.

PP Rawal, chief forest conservator of Gir, says relocation would only mean more inbreeding among the endangered sub-species. 'There is already too much inbreeding. That is why 70 per cent of the cubs do not survive. You need at least 250 pairs for the survival of any species. Right now, we have only 92 males and 100 females in their reproductive years. What sense does it make to separate them further? We must first ensure they propagate and then let them disperse,' he said.

However, several wildlife experts disagree. According to Ravi Chellam, 'The Gujarat government has successfully increased the number of Asiatic lions. But we need to manage that success and think long term. It is better to avoid risk. How would it hurt if just five or eight adults are removed from the population? Their positions are misinformed. They say it is dangerous for the lions to be in tiger territory. But just eight tigers in Kuno pose no grave threat. The lions came to India and settled in the same north-central forests where tigers lived. They coexisted in the past, maintaining an uneasy truce. Lions live in the dry grasslands, whereas tigers move in the thick, dense forest.'

While the disappearance of India's tiger population raises a national outcry, the gentler Asiatic lion's fragile existence does not cause the same alarm. India has 3,000-odd tigers in 27 reserves. But there are only 327 Asiatic lions (according to the last lion census in 2000) confined in only one small sanctuary, Gir.

The Asiatic lion (*Panthera leo persica*) is somewhat different from its African cousin in genetic make-up, skeletal structure and appearance. The Asiatic lion is smaller, has a loose fold on the belly, rarely seen in the African

The Asiatic Gir lions: World's last surviving group of sub-species

Adivasis: Outlaws in their own land

animal, and its mane is less dense. Asiatic lions were once spread across Asia Minor and Arabia; they migrated to India through Persia. In the Indian subcontinent, the range of the Asiatic lions once extended across northern India, as far as Bihar and Orissa in the east, with the Narmada river marking the southern limit. Before the close of the nineteenth century, the Asiatic lion had become extinct everywhere except in Gir. The last lion surviving in the wild outside Saurashtra was reported in 1884.

Ironically, one of the first to rescue the lions from extinction was a *shikari* (hunter) – the Nawab of Junagadh, a princely state in Saurashtra. At the turn of the twentieth century, he was shocked to find that there were only twelve lions left in the grassland. He declared a ban on lion-hunting and ensured that the big cats were protected. After his death, the British administration tried to control hunting in the forest.

The first lion census was conducted in 1936, which put the estimated strength of the lion population at 287. The number dropped to 177 in 1968, because the animal's grassland habitat was shrinking. In 1965, the government started the lion conservation programme and declared the area a sanctuary. Since then, the lion population has been growing steadily. A fresh census is now underway.

Pathak explained why the lions managed to survive in Gir: 'The last few lions remain in Gir because it is a compact, unfragmented ecosystem. And, since the time of the Nawab of Junagadh, there have been continuous conservation efforts here. Moreover, the local people respect nature and our staff works hard to preserve the forest.'

However, conditions for survival are not exactly perfect within the small confines of the Gir sanctuary. Five state highways and a railroad pass through the forest, which also draws 2.5 lakh tourists every year. The three big temples in the forest, which has twenty-three shrines tucked away amid the trees, draw more tourists than the wildlife safaris do. Plus, there is widespread limestone mining in villages just outside the sanctuary, and a cement factory 15 kilometres away from the protected area. This destroys the natural habitat and drains forest resources, including water, very precious during the dry months. Watering holes within the sanctuary are drying up, pushing lions out in search of both water and prey.

Watering holes are also places where it is easier to find prey like deer and nilgai. Recently, lions have fallen into wells in the villages on the outskirts of the forest. Instead of tackling these problems, the government is intent on getting rid of the Maldharis, local herdsmen who have coexisted with the lions in the forest for centuries.

The Maldharis live in small settlements, each called a 'ness'. There were once 129 nesses in the forest. The lions often prey on their cattle, but the Maldharis are not aggressive towards the animals. They accept it as part of nature's cycle. The government offers them Rs 5,000 as compensation, but claiming it entails a long and tedious engagement with the bureaucracy.

In 1972, the government tried to relocate some nesses outside the sanctuary. It shifted 580 of the 845 Maldhari families living in the forest. Though they were given land, the Maldharis did not do well as farmers. Many sold off their land. Today, there are fifty-four nesses (400 families) inside the sanctuary.

Most Maldharis prefer to settle in the forest, even if it means living in small, secluded huts, without minimal amenities like electricity or water supply, and with poor access to markets, schools and hospitals.

Dadhiya ness, which had fifty people, was shifted in the 1970s. Now only twelve families remain. 'We didn't go to the new land, only half our families moved out. The land they gave as compensation was stony, you can't farm on that land,' said Jaggo Ruda Jatwa. 'We have twenty-five heads of cattle, so we stay here. There's nothing for us outside the sanctuary. What will we feed the cattle? We don't know farming.'

The nilgai and the spotted deer or cheetal constitute the main wild prey base of the Asiatic lion.

Pathak says that shifting the Maldharis out of the forest will improve their quality of life and preserve the forest. 'If they live in the forest, it degrades the habitat. Their cattle graze in direct competition with prey like deer.'

But experts question the Forest Department's priorities. 'Relocating the Maldharis is not going to solve the problem. It is more important to translocate the lions,' Ravi Chellam said. 'For the survival of the lions, the Maldharis are not an issue. Lions can coexist with humans. You need to be careful while relocating people. Wildlife conservation need not be purist.'

Both the Maldharis and the trackers, who live in intimate connection with animals, have detailed knowledge of the forest. A tracker who has known the forests long and closely said the lions would not survive without the Maldharis. 'The Maldharis and their livestock are essential to the forest ecosystem. Yes, the cattle eat grass, but without their droppings, how will the grass grow? They are not competing for grazing space with other lion prey like deer, who mainly eat leaves.'

Ravi Chellam, however, believes that the lions can survive without the Maldharis. Lions started feeding more on wild prey (mostly the cheetal) after Maldhari villages relocated and livestock to prey on became scarce. 'Over the years, the number of wild prey animals increased dramatically after some Maldhari villages were relocated and the national park was created. Gradually, the lions have changed from being mainly livestock feeders to wild prey feeders.'

But the tracker insists that the lions prefer livestock even though there are so many more deer now. 'After the Maldharis moved out, the lions also moved beyond the outskirts of the forest because there were more human settlements with cattle there. The last census found fewer lions in the core national park area than in the sanctuary surrounding it.' Ravi Chellam said that the lions are moving out of the sanctuary because of a lack of space rather than food.

As the debate continues on what is best for them, the kings of the jungle seem to be moving out to regain lost territory. If humans cannot make place for them, they seem to be carving out their own spaces, even on the beach. But that alone may not save the species. Some have to be moved much further than the beach.

ALMOST EVERY MONTH, I GET A CALL FROM A FRIEND CALLED Kallan. We don't go much beyond 'hello' because we don't speak the same language. He doesn't know English or Hindi. And I don't know the Sahariya language, Khadi. But, whenever, he gets the chance, Kallan calls from a phone booth in a town two hours away from his village to say 'Namaste'.

Inevitably, he will ask, 'When are you coming here again? The situation is very bad. We are starving.' Each time, I try to get more details, hoping that I can call forest officials to try to get something done. But the language barrier gets in the way.

It's difficult to describe where Kallan lives. His village has shifted so many times – not by choice. It's now called Naya Pipalbaodi (new Pipalbaodi). The old Pipalbaodi was on the banks of a stream in Kuno forest in the Chambal Valley, in north-west Madhya Pradesh. Pipalbaodi is one of twenty-four Sahariya Adivasi villages that were relocated to make way for a lion sanctuary. It was part of a new wildlife conservation idea to translocate five of the last remaining Asiatic lions from their only habitat in the Gir forest in Gujarat, and have a 'second population' in Kuno. This would ensure the survival of the species in case an epidemic hits the Gir lions.

So, 1,545 families were shifted to make way for five lions – who have still not arrived in Kuno. Sounds absurd? Well, it's just the beginning.

The Gujarat government refuses to send any lions outside its boundaries. It wants the Asiatic lions to remain uniquely Gujarati. So, the lions are still thriving in Gir. While people in Kuno have lost everything – their land, their livelihoods and some lives. And, Kuno remains a ghost sanctuary.

The story of how I met Kallan starts not in Kuno, but in Gujarat. I had gone there to research an article on the Asiatic lions in the Gir forest. I thought it was an ironic wildlife conservation story. Most wildlife articles are about species dying out, few remaining. Here, it was the reverse. The population was growing and the Gir National Park was not big enough, so lions were straying out – as far as the coast. Strangely, you could sometimes find lions strolling on a beach.

*Scarred in Gujarat* won Bunsha the Ramnath Goenka Excellence in Journalism Award for non-fiction

As I explored further, the lion translocation story seemed even more bizarre.

I realised that the story about Asiatic lions would not be complete without going to Kuno to see what had happened to the people who had been cleared out for the lions.

Finding them was far more difficult than finding the lions. Telephone connections here are erratic, and after much trying, I managed to get in touch with the only NGO that works there.

The road to Kuno was rough, if you can call it a road. It was a roller coaster ride over the dry, craggy terrain of the Vindhyas, the mountain range that divides north and south India. My first trip was like any other assignment – packed with as many interviews as possible – with people who didn't get land, people who aren't happy with their land, and people who abandoned the resettled village and moved back to their old village.

The residents of Pipalbaodi had moved back to their old village, close to the boundary of the new lion sanctuary. The forest guards pointed us in their direction. That's when I met Kallan. He was with his family – part of the crowd that had come out of their mud huts to tell us their stories. Later, I bumped into Kallan again at the office of the NGO, where he was laughing with embarrassment as he and his friends watched a home video of a recent village festival where he was dancing in a drunken frenzy.

When I returned to Mumbai, I received a fax and some desperate calls from the NGO office telling me that the forest guards forcibly evacuated Pipalbaodi. People had been beaten up, dragged into jeeps, kept in illegal detention for a few days and then dumped at another location. No one knew where this other location was. Two men managed to jump out of the jeep while at Agraa village and went to the NGO to tell them what had happened. The lions would have received better treatment. These are mere adivasis.

I immediately started calling up Forest Department officials, hoping that pressure from the media would ease the pressure on the villagers. The deputy forest conservator told me that 'they were not harassed but they were asked to leave the forest for their own good'. He said, 'We allowed them to grow the mustard crop in the forest. But now they have no work. It's better if they come outside so that we can provide them some employment.'

Next, I called the forest minister. He was disarmingly open and asked me to bring the villagers to meet him. Excited, I called up the head of the NGO (who was now back to HQ in Delhi with no clue to what happened after the urgent fax she sent me) and told her the good news. 'Do you expect us to take them to meet him? That is too much to ask of us,' was her reply. Stunned, I asked, 'Why?' Her answer: 'It may endanger their existence in the area where they are working. And besides, we have tried this in the past and the villagers are too scared to speak in front of the officials.'

It totally bewildered me. Why would an NGO working on this issue and claiming to be a 'third party' in the resettlement process not want to take this chance to make sure the villagers get a hearing? Why didn't they know what had happened to the villagers? 'If we went there, it would endanger their safety further,' was their excuse. 'Let us know when the forest minister wants to meet and we can come and give him a presentation.'

A few days later, I asked the NGO head if I could take the village folk to the forest minister since she was not willing to take them? She couldn't say no.

I had no idea where to start. How do I find where they are now? How do I go there without putting them in any danger of further retaliatory attacks by the forest department? How do I get the villagers from Kuno to Bhopal?

I had to find locals who knew the area. The closest I could get was a farmers' union in Sheopur, the district capital, six hours away. So, we set off in search of Kallan's village. Back on the roller coaster road – both literally and metaphorically.

I realised that my new-found friends at the farmers' union may know the roads, but once we hit the dirt track, they were clueless. So, I had to return to the NGO office. No one was there except Rakesh, the keeper of the chicks. The NGO raises poultry and distributes chicks to villagers as part of the UN's 'Livelihood Program'. Rakesh had no clue what had happened to Pipalbaodi. The villagers could have fallen off the map, for all he cared.

We asked around, took a local with us in the jeep and headed for the old village. We parked behind a tree before the sanctuary's entrance gate and made him walk to see if the villagers were there. Not a soul in sight. So, he took us to the new village. On a very long, rocky dirt track – very hot, dusty and bumpy.

Finally when we reached, there was just a small settlement of families dumped in the midst of this dry, barren landscape. I asked them if they would be afraid to speak to the minister. There were so many willing to come with me to Bhopal that they had to go through a process of elimination. Only three could fit in the back of the car, but they wanted to squeeze in four. Then, there was a scramble to find clothes. They went through each house, looking for pants they could borrow to wear for the meeting.

While I waited for them to get ready, the others showed me around the 'resettlement site'. It was arid and hard stone. Nothing could grow there. There wasn't even enough drinking water, and the little that existed was contaminated. The village was so far from anything that they had to migrate to find work.

The tyranny of the Forest Department was even worse than I had imagined. They kept the villagers illegally at Pohri forest headquarters and let two people go back to the village, threatening that only when they made sure that the entire village had evacuated the forest would they release the others in custody. The villagers had no choice. They had to leave. The NGO did not do anything to help. Not even a few chicks were thrown their way.

Back on the road. This time a long, twelve-hour drive to Bhopal, the state capital. When the forest minister met us, Kallan and his friends explained the problem to him clearly and without hesitation. The minister then instructed the chief conservator of forests to take action. As we left the office, and I said goodbye at the bus stand (it was their first trip outside their village), I started wondering if this crazy journey was really going to help them.

Luckily, the next week, the bureaucrat was in Kuno to take stock of the situation. The villagers demanded fertile land, but the official said that there wasn't any better land available. Instead, the Forest Department would try to improve the soil quality of the land by digging through the rocky terrain. Access to a new school was assured. Neither worked out. The state can't even give them what was promised in the rehabilitation plan. There isn't enough fertile land in the region. Did anyone think of that in the hurry to get them out?

Funnily enough, the Kuno project was considered one in which there was 'successful rehabilitation with the consent of the oustees'. *Sanctuary*, India's premier wildlife magazine even gave the forest officer in charge of the rehabilitation an award for 'Earth Heroes' at the *Sanctuary* Wildlife Awards 2002. Well, he got rid of the people, didn't he? Mission accomplished.

Doing this story has been like watching a theatre of the absurd unfold over several years across varying landscapes with the most bizarre twists. It was a lesson on how wildlife conservation works on the ground – beyond the pages of government reports and glossy wildlife magazines. It's a world we have inherited from the British sahibs who created protected forests and outlawed Adivasis from their own lands. Our brown sahibs continue the tradition. The laws and decisions are made by people from the cities. They call the Adivasis who have lived in and preserved forests for centuries 'the encroachers'– who are 'illegal' and have to be 'removed'.

Regardless of the kind of forest/landscape or the peculiarities of each individual situation or region, a uniform law is applied to all. It's a rigid approach that doesn't help conservation, because it doesn't consider the complexities of each situation and doesn't involve local people in the planning process. So, it inevitably leads to the deprivation and alienation of people.

India has more than 600 protected areas (PAs), occupying almost 5 per cent of the country's land area. Around three to four million people live inside these PAs and several million more in adjacent areas. Their lives are intricately linked to the forest and they depend on natural resources for their basic needs. Precise figures on the number of people evicted from PAs are not available (itself an indication of the casual way in which this has been treated by state and central governments), but research by environmentalist Ashish Kothari estimates that it might be around 100,000. But are they really the ones destroying our forests and its wildlife? Or is it the poachers, mining, quarrying, logging, power projects and tourist resorts catering to the greed of the city slickers?

Is it possible to preserve forests without destroying the people who are part of it? Does it have to be one or the other? A small, influential wildlife conservation lobby clings on to the old dogma. But the world has moved on. International organisations like the UN and the International Union for Conservation of Nature (IUCN) believe in community conservation, that people are an integral part of conservation. The concept is as old as the hills in India. We have a wealth of ancient sacred groves and lakes that are guarded, regulated and preserved entirely by communities, who have an intimate knowledge of their environment.

In the last decade, the forest department has started involving communities in forest management. In most cases, it has been far more successful than total state control. For example, in Periyar Tiger Reserve in Kerala, a few enlightened forest officers involved local communities in starting an eco-tourism programme where locals are the trekking guides. This has curbed smuggling of timber and poaching, and there has been an increase in wild animal populations. Moreover, the women formed a voluntary '*Vasant Sena*' (Spring Army) to patrol the forest. Their motivation: 'We do this for our children ... if the forest does not survive, how will we?'

Sadly, these are the exception, not the norm. Most forest dwellers in India are considered outlaws in their own land. Several are denied access to collect even berries, fruit and other minor forest produce like *tendu* leaves (which is their only source of income). That's why their tribes and cultures are dying with the forest. The Sahariyas (meaning 'residents of the jungle') are one of India's oldest and poorest tribes, and live in the most remote interiors of the country. The resettlement made their distress even more acute by depriving them of their only means of income – gathering forest produce. In 2005, several children died of malnutrition-related illnesses in some of the 'resettled' villages. But no one batted an eyelid. If a lion dies in Gir, it is national news. When children die in Kuno, it rarely touches the media.

Kallan's survival is on the line. The last time he called, he told me, 'There's a wedding in the village. *Hum log dhoom macha rahe hai* (We are partying). When are you coming?' I haven't gone back. It wouldn't change a thing. The change will come from people sitting in air-conditioned offices (who rarely venture outside). They will decide his fate. That's why Kallan keeps calling me. Hoping that I can get through to them. To try to make sure he doesn't remain a voice in the wilderness.

GAUTAM **BHIMANI**

Gautam Bhimani, 32, is presenter/commentator with ESPN Star Sports.

**THE AWARD WINNER**
SPORTS JOURNALISM, BROADCAST

# LIVING ON THE EDGE

GAUTAM BHIMANI REVISITS SOME OF HIS EXPERIENCES AS A SPORTS PRESENTER, SOME BEYOND THE CALL OF DUTY. HIS STORIES PRESENT THE DRAMA OF LIVING ON THE EDGE.

RIGHT IN THE HEART OF TERROR-STRUCK ZIMBABWE. LESS than 300 yards from Robert Mugabe's front door.

It was my very first overseas tour with ESPN Star and I had been sent primarily as a news reporter with a few additional duties to provide player and coach interviews for the live telecast. Having finished my chats on the first morning of the Harare Test with John Wright, Sourav Ganguly and Heath Streak for the day, I was at a bit of a loose end and wandered over to explore the ground. The centrepiece of the stadium was a pub called the Keg and Maiden.

I propped myself on a bar stool, ordered myself a lemonade and a plate of steak and chips since I was still on duty and settled down to watch the game. The guys at the next table had ordered themselves a *'giraffe'* (five litres of beer in a tall slim-necked pitcher), which was the Keg special. Sachin was settling down to author another Sachin Special. I thought to myself, does watching test cricket get any better? Gorgeous blue skies. A near-perfect 17 degrees centigrade. Sitting at a pub digging into a juicy steak just inches from the boundary line. Lager and conversation flowing. And the world's best batsman on show.

It was enough for me to want to do a story on this. This was not part of the script or part of my job profile but I could not resist. My producer resisted but put that story on air. A few hours later, an urgent memo from the boss. Could I get him another similar story for lunch day two. And another on day three. And ...

So, frivolous as it may sound, that tryst with a pitcher of mildly intoxicating amber fluid was the springboard to seven years of reporting from the edge of the boundary. Seven years of actually living on the edge!

I have never been faced with the realities of being on the battlefront but in the context of sport I have done a few stupid things in the line of duty. And most of them out of choice. I have reported from the top of a giant tree in the Caribbean, taken *panga* with a fierce Maori warrior in New Zealand and swum with deadly stingrays in Queensland. Colourful, entertaining, sometimes great fun, but dangerous too (my wife Rashi and son Raag are usually more petrified than I am). I thought I would choose my favourite three 'misadventures' to highlight what my typical day at the office often entails.

## DIZZYING HEIGHTS

The Melbourne Cricket Ground is a mesmerising amphitheatre like no other. Getting a birds' eye view was another thrill altogether. I had gone to the very last row of the top-tier of the gigantic Southern Stand and got a vertigo view

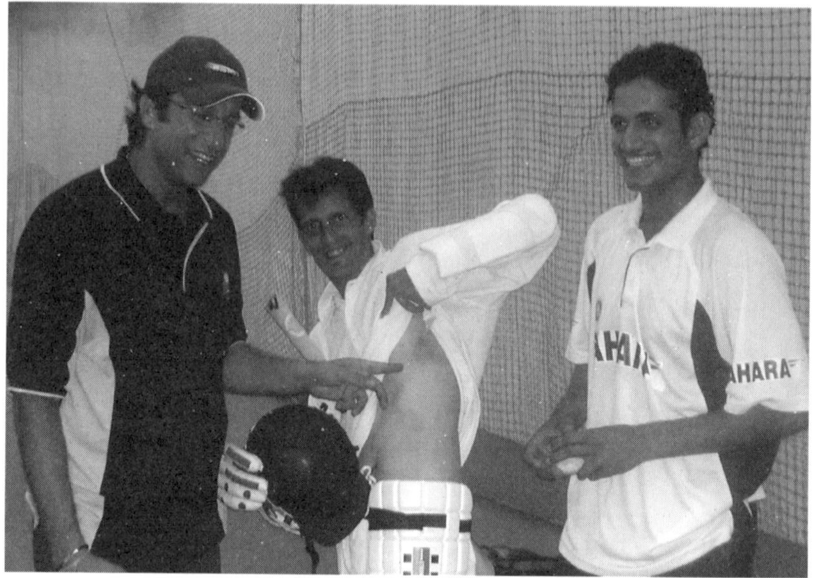


Getting the story the hard way: Gautam Bhimani with Wasim Akram and Irfan Pathan

of the arena. But something was missing. I wanted to get an even better vantage point. I looked skywards at the 130-tonne floodlight towers. They just happened to be the world's highest cricket floodlight towers. Climbing up there? Surely not!

The paperwork arrived swiftly. Indemnity clauses to sign. Insurance papers to produce. This venture was at my own risk. I was responsible for any mishap. Yes, yes. Now get on with it. Oh, it also took some convincing to get my cameraman Rajneesh to agree to climb up there with me. Remember, he also had the minor detail of a camera to take up with him. We arrived at the base of Tower 1 and I began groping for the lift switch on the exterior. The caretaker looked at me mighty strangely. 'Gotta walk up, mate.' He appeared to get a sadistic pleasure out of saying that. Either that, or it was his way of discouraging visitors to the tower.

The staircase was like a series of ladders inside a dark tunnel placed vertically with narrow platforms every twenty steps or so. There were a total of thirteen landings to negotiate before we reached our destination. This got narrower as we went higher and higher. The diameter at the base of the tower was 4.2 metres and at the top a mere 2 metres! By now we had reached a staggering height of 75 metres (approximately twenty-five floors). At the very top was another narrow platform gantry where technicians come to check and change the gigantic bulbs that were now at eye level. Each individual metal halide lamp is a whopping 2,000 watts. Each tower has approximately 140 lamps (a total of 844 in the six towers), making the total output from our tower alone a staggering 2,80,000 watts! Now I know why they go on and on about the charged-up atmosphere at the MCG!

If it was possible to dwarf the MCG, we had just done it.

So transfixed was I by the magnificent view all around me, I nearly forgot the real reason I had come up there. It took a gentle reminder from Rajneesh's sore shoulder (lugging his giant 13 kilogram Betacam all the way up the vertical tunnel) to swing me back in action with the microphone. It was a case of Camera. Action. And plenty of Lights!

## A RIB-TICKLING TALE

How often does one receive a sickening blow to the rib cage, get completely winded and out of breath, not be able to sleep on that side for months afterwards but still come out cherishing that moment for a lifetime? Well, probably only once in a lifetime. And possible if that blow comes from a man who has taken 952 international wickets. And if the receiver of the blow happens to be someone who will never get a chance to play international cricket, facing a bowling legend is a rare privilege. This is the strange tale of the day I temporarily lost my mind and decided to take on Wasim Akram at his game on his territory.

I had picked up the Pakistani fast bowling legend and India's latest swing sensation Irfan Pathan from the hotel and driven them to the nets at the 'Gabba' in Brisbane. Irfan wanted a few bowling tips and was hanging on to every word like a wide-eyed fifth grader attending his first senior coaching class.

I also had to do a story with Wasim. The peg being that Mr Akram is rather peeved at the fact that I was beating him handsomely at our net-based fantasy game Super Selector, and as a result he has challenged me to face him at the nets to show me what 'real cricket' is all about.

With everything in place, I began padding up. 'Where's your chest guard?' someone taunted. Hmmm, good point, I thought, and trudged off to the Indian dressing room. Anil Kumble had not reached. He was one guaranteed source of a chest guard. Never mind, I thought. I will just tell Wasim to bowl me a few harmless deliveries outside off stump.

The cameras were set up. Wasim Akram had a brand new red cherry in his hand. I took a leg stump guard from umpire Irfan Pathan. Adjusted my helmet strap. Nervously fiddled with the Velcro strap on my right pad. And settled to face the first delivery, feeling every bit like a goldfish in a shark's tank. And here was the shark running in towards me.

I barely saw the first four deliveries and finally on the fifth ball I planted my left foot down the wicket and made contact in the middle of the bat. I held the pose to make sure the cameraman caught it. I was not certain the bowler was all that pleased at getting driven in this manner. I noticed he took a couple of extra steps for the next ball. That is one of the last things I remembered vividly as Akram, with an extra spring in his step, ran in and banged in the next one. The next few moments were a blur. The ball was short, rising rapidly and pitched on leg stump. Instinct and years of watching television told me to rock on to the back foot and pull it viciously or maybe move back and across and fend it off. Ducking was a third option. But this was no time for options. As my mind grappled with these choices, it hardly noticed the sound of a dull thud. The distinct dull thud of a leather cricket ball making rapid contact with the human ribcage.

I was down in a heap. Gasping for breath. I could hear distant voices. Cries of 'water' and 'ice' were vaguely audible. It was several minutes before I could sit up and come to terms with what was going on. The first concern I expressed was to the cameraman. 'Did you get it all?' I asked. Surely this pain had been worth something!

I finally had the courage to look down at the wound. It was an ugly purple. The size of a cricket ball. Every breath I took was agony. I could not sleep on my left side for months. But hey, I had my story!

AERIAL ADVENTURE

Commentary boxes round the world differ a great deal, be it in size, shape, location, temperature or height. You name it. But ironically the most cramped commentary box I have ever encountered is also by far the most memorable.

The Antigua Test in 2002 on a bowler's graveyard was fast heading for a dull draw. Simon Wheeler, who was directing the TWI-produced telecast, summoned me to ask if I had ever done commentary from a chopper. I informed him that I had never even been up in a chopper in my life.

To make matters worse, just minutes before we were off the ground, the local assistant, a massive six-foot-six Jamaican with two gold teeth called Steve, made my initiation ceremony more dramatic! He was giving the bird last-minute touch-ups and began yanking hard at the door. Surely it would open more gently than that. Moments later, much to my horror, the door came off in his hand. Whoops, there goes my helicopter debut, I thought.

Next thing I see him with a huge grin on his face, gold teeth glinting in the midday sun, walking around to the other side and pulling off that door as well! Hmmm, what sort of sabotage was this? Seeing my concern, Steve walks up to me, a chopper door in each hand, saying, 'Don worree maan, Can't have doors on dees. You take camera, how you shoot from eenside closed door?'

Good point. Logical. Far from sensible.

Gautam Bhimani with a Maori Warrior in New Zealand

Before I could change my mind, we were strapped in and airborne. The pilot in front, the camera and the cameraman and I jostling for space in the back seat. Taking off was the strangest feeling. Like some giant invisible hand had reached down and picked up the helicopter and lifted it straight up in the air. If there were still any apprehensions lurking within me, I think I must have left them on the helipad along with bits of my stomach, as the moment we were 500 feet in the air, the view (and not the fear) took my breath away. It was the stuff one watches and envies on channels like Travel & Living. Here I was on my travels, living every bit of it.

Minutes after being airborne, we headed out to sea, almost skimming the surface of the gorgeous blue waters. The water was so crystal clear that the ocean floor was a sight to behold.

Soon, I heard the reassuring voice of the director Simon coming through, loud and clear. The stadium was in full view below us. At the start of the next over I heard Michael Holding hand it over to the chopper and I was on. We circled over the ground as I did my best to describe the action happening below. I followed the cameraman's lead and, after checking that my strap and seat belt were on tight, I too peeped out for a better view. The wind whistled through the open door helicopter, making it that much tougher to pick up the voice of the director and the commentators coming through the tight-fitting headphones.

A flighted delivery: Commentary from a chopper

The commentary team changed down on earth and I heard the familiar voice of Sir Vivian Richards. He egged me on to describe the view. This was rather nerve racking as I was now interacting with someone who was already a legend, and to make matters worse, Antigua was his home island. I had only explored Antigua for four days. Along with my brief experience, I summoned up all the homework I had done, with my *Lonely Planet* readings.

I was desperate to pinch myself to wake up from what had to be a dream, but decided it was too risky to make sudden movements. Why bother? After all, it wasn't a dream. At that moment, I was determined to enjoy every second of that dream flight. Within twenty minutes, I would come down to earth, literally and metaphorically.

HIRAL **SACHDE**

Hiral Sachde, 25, is Special Correspondent with CNBC TV 18.

THE AWARD WINNERS
BUSINESS AND ECONOMIC JOURNALISM, BROADCAST

# BENAMI PAN CARD

AN ADVERTISEMENT ON CHEAP PAPER PLASTERED ON A RAILWAY BRIDGE LEADS A CURIOUS JOURNALIST TO TRACK THIS STORY OF BENAMI PAN CARDS.

BELIEVE IT OR NOT, I GOT THE BENAMI PAN CARD STORY FROM a local train. When I saw an anonymous advertisement on cheap paper plastered illegally on a railway overbridge in suburban Mumbai – PAN card and a number – my instinct told me it should not to be ignored. I took the number down and placed a call as soon as I reached office. I had thought this was going to turn out different than regular news or trend stories, what I didn't know was that it would go on to be an award-winning story.

It pays to be observant. And after being a journalist you pick up a lot of things, like reading a document upside down from across the table or overhearing conversations while travelling – not with ulterior motives. It just helps you keep abreast with developments you might have missed.

So here I was with a story facing the regular where-do-I-start problem. Next step was to take the hidden camera and meet 'the advertiser'. I got an alias. I decided to pose as a tuition teacher from Gujarat – wish my ethnic background was not obvious from my looks and I could have faked something else. I reached this easy-to-lose-place in Dadar in the heart of Mumbai. It was a commercial premise with little cubbyholes for different offices – I was welcomed by a street-smart secretary to the 'sir'– mastermind Rahul Kamble who ran this business. She asked me my name. 'Parul, why do you want a PAN card,' she asked me. 'I stay here with my maternal uncle, I need to buy a house of my own and I want to apply for a loan.' 'Do you have any documents?' 'No, I am from Ahmedabad, I lost them all in the earthquake,' I tried to be as convincing as possible. (I always wonder if I could have an alternate career as a fiction writer.)

An investigative story is a mind game. Spontaneity is its rule number one. It is fun to watch how you can lie like it's the only truth in that moment. You may be daunted by the fact that you are such a convincing liar. But it's a necessary evil. You have to protect your identity till you achieve your goal. In my earlier assignment that involved mystery shopping for mutual funds, I posed as an NRI investor, with an accent, wanting to make quick gains.

After spending about half an hour with the unauthorised PAN agent, I left. And as I was about to save the file on the spy camera, I hit the wrong button and lost it all. I was disappointed and scared – what would I tell my editor. How would I go back and get it all again? That's another hazard of television – visuals lost is story lost. However, that was not the only technical glitch that we faced.

Obviously my editor was miffed with the incident and Khushboo was co-assigned to help me with spy cams. So Parul and her friend 'Anita' both wanted a PAN card now. We went again and this time – bingo – along with the woman we had the man himself on our spy camera.

Rahul Kamble was a typical product of our urban lifestyle. He seemed like a college dropout powered by the local political flunkies. Slightly filmy – inspired by none other than Vijay Dinanath Chauhan (Amitabh Bachchan's character in *Agneepath*) – the way he walked and talked, his clothes said that he knew he was doing something not very legal but he had no qualms about it. A lot of people do such things in Mumbai. The city is bursting at the seams with immigrants from all over the country. And nobody would complain about a man like Kamble who can get them a bonafide certificate from a local MLA, a PAN card and even a loan for a price ranging from Rs 500 to Rs 5,000.

A lot of people associate risk with investigative journalism. It's true to a certain extent. You are dealing with someone who does not understand scruples. Rahul Kamble was certainly not the kind who could kill but he was capable of causing harm. After our second visit he tried to be overfriendly. He offered to assist Khushboo in finding a home in Navi Mumbai. We were far from happy at his overtures. I was cautious of my movements through those two months that we took to do this story. Khushboo, too, was advised to be cautious. I used to take the same route to travel home each day and bumping into Kamble might make him suspicious.

Kamble told us that he usually avoids dealing with female clients. 'They are very inquisitive' he said. The reason he was helping me? Well, I was this destitute girl, living with a devilish uncle, desperately seeking help. And my friend was an extended business opportunity. She also wanted a loan. I strengthened my case by telling him that my uncle would hold me accountable for the Rs 500 that I was paying him and in return got an assurance from Kamble that I would get my money's worth.

For all their fun and thrills, spy camera shoots are very taxing. My suggestion is, two people work better than one. Handling the camera, talking and thinking all at the same time can be a draining exercise. And in case it's a female reporter then it's more convincing – women seek company to even go buying vegetables, so how would one go shopping for a PAN card by herself? Also, it always helps to keep the subject busy. He won't get suspicious and if he does and you are in danger, your colleague can be your moral support.

So the PAN card was applied for. There was another interesting sub-plot to our story. The rule says that in the absence of identity proofs and documents you have to get a certificate of identity signed by a member of parliament, MLA or a municipal councillor or a gazetted officer. You do not need original documents as per the IT rules just a certified copy is enough. It's the two PAN issuing agencies – National Stock Depository Limited (NSDL) and UTI Technology Services Limited (UTI TSL) that accept applications duly filled. They forward it to the IT department that in turn allots a PAN number. The agencies then forward the PAN card to the applicant.

We then set out to find the MLA 'Prabhakar Vishwas Khade' supposedly belonging to Peasants and Workers Party (I bet you are reading about this party for the first time here). A source at the Vidhan Bhavan in Mumbai helped us in our search. Armed with Marathi – the local language of Maharashtra – that opens most gates in the bureaucratic set up, I went through booklets of the list of MLAs and MPs that are and have been. Search result: negative. Prabhakar Vishwas Khade not found. The man who was supposed to sign my character certificate did not exist.

We contacted the PWP representative in Mumbai. He confirmed our doubts. There was no Prabhakar Vishwas Khade associated with the party ever. The letterhead that was to go as my identity proof document with the PAN application was not authentic. But the application was accepted without any questions and I was allotted a number.

No investigative story can ever be released without speaking to all parties involved. There is no room for mistakes or slip ups. It can not only cost you your job but also your credibility. The wait for the PAN card was longer than expected. Our application was being processed through UTI TSL. After a meeting with the CEO of UTI TSL, he agreed to speak to us on record. An appointment for an on-camera interview was scheduled for the next day. UTI TSL is based in Navi Mumbai, which is an hour and a quarter from central Mumbai where our office is situated. We did the interview, but to our dismay it couldn't be used as it had audio glitches.

We were less than two days away from our deadline. We still had to speak to the chief commissioner of IT, Mumbai, redo the interview with UTI TSL and the PAN card was still not in our hands. It was mailed to the fake address that we had given in the application. We back-tracked the PAN card with the help of UTI TSL. A rider was rushed to collect it from the courier company based in a far suburb of Mumbai. On the same day we interviewed the IT commissioner and UTI TSL head. We had also contacted the Ministry of Finance for their official response.

Television is a time-consuming medium. Three days in a row I had to travel a minimum of three hours each day for a ten minute interview with UTI TSL. You need more than just spy cams. Investigative stories are a challenge as far as visuals go. That's why most of them have to be backed up with reconstructions or dramatised sequences.

It does not end here. We have to compile these visuals with audio, music, special effects to make it a half-hour televised show. The process known as editing takes at least twenty-four hours throughout which the producer and the reporter have to be present. Prior to the edit you have to cull out relevant visuals and sound bites from a mound of tapes. That saves time on the edit table. And as we were about to close the episode we got a response from the Ministry of Finance. The final tape was submitted two and a half hours prior to the telecast. That's the edge-of-a-seat life we all live in television. The passion and pride in our work kept us going through it all.

In television reporting teamwork is mandatory and respecting your colleagues comes more out of habit than mandate. Khushboo worked relentlessly to make this story happen. I can't imagine my Benami PAN card story happening without her. Whether it is a cameraperson and a technical assistant who shoots visuals for you or the editor who sits up all night with you to bring out the episode, they all put in their best just like you. You have your producer – in our case our colleague Natasha Thomas – who decides the treatment of the story and final output. A producer makes a story telecast-worthy. We had a supportive team that was backing us up while we were in the field. We were lucky and grateful to have them. Last but not the least it was our editor – Vivek Law – who believed in us and motivated us throughout.

The Ramnath Goenka Excellence in Journalism Award also belongs to all these people behind the scenes who stood by us throughout.

Amidst all this success, I must admit that I had failed as a daughter. I had promised my father before I joined this profession that I would never cover crime or politics. He feared for my safety and wanted to be sure that his little girl was safe in the big bad world. I had turned down the offer of being a full-time reporter on the investigative crime show *Uncovered* more than once but I did contribute to the show every time I got a chance. Ironically, breaking that promise has given me recognition and credibility. And now my father is the happiest and proudest of all.

After the story was released, the illegal PAN agents were raided. But Kamble had escaped. The finance ministry met up with NSDL and UTI TSL to discuss changes in the PAN issuing process. But concrete action is not yet taken.

And that's how I got a benami PAN card again after a year, with a fake name and birth certificate. This time the agents had managed to submit ration card copies with our names. Both agencies highlighted the fact that the rules were set by the IT department and Ministry of Finance. They have no right or power to ask for original documents even for verification.

As I look at my Ramnath Goenka Excellence in Journalism trophy, I only hope that the Finance Minister P Chidambaram introduces biometric PAN cards. He mentioned this to us in person at the award ceremony last year.

Finally, a suggestion to all budding journalists – keep your eyes and ears open. It may happen to you too. One busy day the overbridge that you have taken a thousand times earlier can lead you to a path-breaking story that would not just earn you professional excellence but also make you feel complete as a journalist.

KHUSHBOO **NARAYAN**

Khushboo Narayan, 25, is staff writer with *MINT-HT* and *Wall Street Journal*.

## PERSONAL ACCOUNT

I THINK OUR BIG STORY WAS SO OBVIOUS THAT IT WENT unnoticed. We got our story from Borivali station, in suburban Mumbai. Eye-catching advertisements offering assistance to people who didn't have a Permanent Account Number, or PAN card, were posted at several places near the station. The cryptic advertisement was so obvious that no one noticed the scam brewing in it.

As journalists we are taught to be observant so that we spot and expose what those in authority, or otherwise, may decide to gloss over. The PAN card exposé was one such attempt to awaken the authorities to the potential misuse of the unique identity card required for any financial transaction.

I strongly believe that truth sometimes has a strange way of finding its way into the public domain, and in this case it was an obscure advertisement. When we started working on the story, my co-reporter Hiral and I were convinced that it was not going to be an easy task. Any credible news report required facts to back it. We had to thoroughly investigate the issue and get to the root of the scam before we could make it public. We wanted to present an unbiased report of an economic crime that was being perpetrated by unscrupulous people. While doing the story we double-checked all the information we had, to ensure that we did not misrepresent facts.

I can never forget our first visit to one PAN card shop run by a man named Rahul Kamble. He operated out of a 10 sq ft room hidden in one of the lanes of Dadar West; it had just enough space for two people to fit in. We decided to pose as immigrants in need of PAN cards to secure a bank loan. At this point a single bad move would have spoilt the operation and our chance to expose the scam. We cooked up a teary story about our lives and convinced him to get us PAN cards. In the very first meeting we had accomplished a lot.

The Act that governs the issuance of PAN card lists a number of documents that needs to be submitted along with the application form. In case an applicant doesn't have any documents, they can get a certificate of identity signed by a member of parliament, MLA, or a municipal councillor or a gazetted officer. The biggest loophole in the law is that an applicant doesn't need to submit original documents; a certified copy is good enough. We had identified the loophole that was going to be used by our tout for us. It was certain that these agents had their business partners in the administration.

What appalled me was the confidence with which the crime was being committed. This agent established himself as a magician who could make PAN cards out of paper scraps.

Another tout who used to dole out PAN cards to people who were willing to pay, displayed the same confidence. I think the only difference between the two was their service charge. While the former charged Rs 500 per card, the latter demanded Rs 1,500 because he had a bigger office that was located in the up-market area of the city.

It is true that investigative reporting is dangerous because there is always a chance of getting caught. My former editors, colleagues and parents have always asked me to exercise caution while dealing with fraudsters. But as an investigative reporter what worried me the most was the lost chance of exposing a scam due to inaccuracies in reportage. Also, when a reporter works on an investigative story he/she is overloaded with information but it's imperative to identify and pick the most important information and discard others.

A few days into the investigation and we knew the nexus ran deep. Money buys everything and these agents in connivance with certain officials were making the most out of the loopholes in the system. I feel that there is great space for corruption and crime in our system most of which goes unpunished. Maybe that is the reason why India ranks lowest in Transparency International ratings.

In our subsequent visits to these agents we happened to meet a 'regular' applicant because he had applied for a PAN card, for a fourth time. Our agent Kamble's regular customer was a fraudster too; he had used his fake identities to get the PAN card. His business was to use these cards to borrow money from various banks and later default on loan repayments.

While doing a story, it is extremely important for any journalist to establish contact with all the parties involved. And the most difficult part of our story was to get the public authorities to react to the issue. Mostly when the media exposes the loopholes in the system, the public authorities try to cover up rather than take a proactive stance. There is always a fear that it might throw open a can of worms in the public domain.

After much effort we did manage to draw the attention of the public authorities. We were working against a strict deadline and the moment we thought that we could conclude the story, we were faced with a problem – an audio glitch in the interview of a senior official of UTI Technology Services Limited (UTI TSL). UTI TSL is one of the two agencies that accepts PAN card applications, the other being National Stock Depository Limited (NSDL).

As a television journalist it is essential to ensure the best quality of video. With the help of our team of young reporters and producers it was possible to re-shoot the interview.

In India, investigative journalism is often wrongly referred to as spy camera journalism but there is much more to it than just hidden cameras. People feel that journalists or media houses, which encourage 'sting operations', propagate sensationalism and probably feed on it. Sting operations are not always a means to garner viewership ratings. At the same time I believe that it can be easily misused: we have seen both the faces of sting operations. The Tehelka exposé which rocked the nation with its chilling revelations of murky defence deals and then the ugly side of sting operations when a schoolteacher in Delhi was falsely implicated in a flesh trade case. I believe it depends on the journalist as well as the publication to ensure that this powerful tool is not misused.

The story ran on our channel and soon the income-tax officials conducted raids in the city. Some touts were arrested while others went into hiding. The government announced its plan to tighten PAN card issuance norms and called for a high-level meeting to review the entire process. But this superficial commotion did not last for long and the problem was not uprooted.

Sadly, even a year later, nothing has been done to block the gaping holes in the issuance process of PAN cards. We ran yet another series on agents who were forging documents to get PAN cards. This time the concerned authorities shrugged off their responsibility and blamed each other for the failure. At this point there was no respite from the frustration and disappointment. A few months later we were awarded the Ramnath Goenka Excellence in Journalism Award. During the award ceremony we met the finance minister who assured us that by October 2007 biometric PAN cards would be introduced which will eliminate frauds.

October 2007 came and went, I quit my job at Network 18 and joined another organisation but to date nothing has changed except the sudden rise in the number of advertisements offering assistance for making PAN cards. The question that remains unanswered is – what is the government waiting for?

The one thing I have learnt in the short span of my career is that a reporter's job is to relentlessly report on issues that concern the public at large and help uphold democracy.

I would not disagree with people who find today's journalism too market-oriented, since we are often forced to cover issues of mass appeal. But for me the biggest battle is to survive in this new era of journalism while sticking to my ethics and striving to make socially relevant issues appealing to the masses. The award has appreciated our work and encouraged me to pursue my passion with further determination.

## KISHALAY **BHATTACHARJEE**

Kishalay Bhattacharjee, 40, is Bureau Chief, North East, NDTV.

**THE AWARD WINNER**
REGIONAL AWARD, NORTHEAST, BROADCAST

# HUMAN RIGHTS AND HUMAN WRONGS

KISHALAY BHATTACHARJEE VISITS THE CAMPS OF DISPLACED ADIVASIS IN ASSAM AND REPORTS A HEART-WRENCHING TALE OF 'HUMAN RIGHTS AND HUMAN WRONGS', OF CITIZENS DISPLACED IN THEIR OWN COUNTRY.

I WISH REPORTS CHANGED LIVES. REPORTS CHANGED SITUATIONS. I wish two years after my report on internally displaced people in lower Assam their condition had changed. It has only worsened.

It's only incidental that I sat to write this account when the country celebrated its 59th Republic Day. But it's not incidental that while the bugle blows from the heart of India's capital honouring the bravehearts, thousands of Indians barely enjoy basic rights.

Our journey to the camps of displaced people began with this thought: why should citizens be denied their rights? Besides this question, one that remains unanswered, what stayed with me are moments filtered down after an 'extempore' shoot. Let me explain why.

I think it was in the manner in which we shot the report. We shot for four hours and produced a half hour report. However, we told the news editor and the producer that we had shot for three days. They wouldn't be convinced that a four-hour shoot would be good enough to produce a half-hour special.

It was a hot summer day. We took the Rajdhani Express from Guwahati and arrived at Kokrajhar town. It is a rundown, dusty township which is more accustomed to hostility than peace.

The only available private vehicle on hire was an almost vintage red Maruti which took us to and around the Adivasi camps. That is when we confronted the misery of the human condition of a community huddled into these makeshift camps for a decade.

For years I have been carrying with me a copy of a journal, *Refugees*. Maybe for its pictures. Maybe for the images that the word conjures up in my mind. But here in the midst of thousands of refugees, I became speechless.

The global refugee tragedy has only deepened with the proliferation of civil wars and ethnic riots and the creation of another class of dispossessed people, the so called 'internally displaced'.

Refugees are generally those who flee persecution in their home country and seek safety in a second state. As such they receive international protection and help. Internally displaced people abandon their homes for similar human rights abuses but remain in their own land. They receive only ad hoc assistance and are not protected by international law.

I called the report 'Human Rights and Human Wrongs'. It highlights rights, which are still being denied, wrongs that are still perpetrated.

The camps were unhygienic. From time to time agencies have done their bit to set up tube wells, schools, community kitchens but most of them are abandoned now.

Living with the gun: Women and children are the worst sufferers

We moved through the camps recording anger and frustration. At every location emerged from dirty alleys, crowds of children with hungry faces, to speak to the camera about their condition, always reminding my cameraperson that we were running against time.

One of our destinations was a ceasefire camp of a small militant group – the Adivasi Cobra Force.

These plains of lower Assam bordering Bangladesh have lived through two of the bloodiest insurgencies of this region. Ironically, today one of them runs a democratically elected autonomous council, the other in a ceasefire with the Government of India lives in designated camps.

There was, however, a third insurgent outfit born out of the worst ethnic riots in this region between the indigenous Bodos and the Santhali settlers in which 15,000 people were killed or have disappeared.

In the camp of the Adivasi Cobra Force, a group of young men were getting ready for lunch. They had a few guns and sets of bows and arrows which they traditionally carry with them. They didn't appear hostile. After the refugee camps, the condition in which the ceasefire camp was being run did not surprise me. The food was inedible, the living conditions, miserable.

After constructing sequences of the young fighters taking their targets (to my camera's delight) we wanted to complete our visit to the remaining camps. There weren't many camps, but there were many voices.

Ten years of Bodo militancy and revenge killings have made it virtually impossible for these Adivasis to return to their homes. Those who have, live in fear. The others in uncertainty. Over 12,000 families have been sent home. But in a chilling symmetry of figures there are still over a lakh trying to put their lives back together and get even the most basic amenities and rights any human being deserves.

So far, they have no land, no jobs, no food.

Our progress through these camps was not welcomed with great enthusiasm. The people here have had their share of visitors with cameras who they know would fetch them virtually nothing.

In our hurried treks through the camps emerged another image – a more powerful image – that of the invisible generation, the lost generation. Someone like Wilson who was born in the refugee camp. There were thousands of minor children in these camps, many of them born in sub-human conditions lacking even basic health care.

The majority of refugees in the world are children. That is the case here too. But while their numbers swell, children have been largely ignored as a specific group. There are no records of how many children have died in these camps. The ones who survive are dropping out of childhood, forced into labour.

There has been darkness here for too long. Eighteen-year-old Badki looks much older than her age. Around 200 people from this camp have disappeared. Many have lost their sanity.

Before we raced to catch our train we witnessed the most enduring of images of human existence. Somewhere in all the misery, there are signposts of hope. In Serfanguri, people were slowly beginning to look forward rather than backwards. We were forced to join a colourful dance where the women go round in a very happy rhythm and the men play the music in the backdrop.

Our story was done. There were many stories in one story.

This is how I do most of my reports. It appears rushed. But I can't linger over my shoots. I try capturing moments and images and let them tell the story. Juxtaposed with the spontaneous reactions of people. Nothing is staged here. No lines are rehearsed. Each frame of the story should give an impression of the larger picture.

When we returned with unreserved tickets on some Guwahati-bound night train, I wasn't sure whether we had got the real story.

A year later I travelled to the same camps. No one recognised me there. The faces were unfamiliar to me as well. Moni, a fifteen-year-old girl had just escaped from a Delhi house after she was sold thrice. There's more anger and

Years of Bodo militancy and revenge killings have made it impossible for the Adivasis to return to their homes

helplessness. There are many more stories waiting to be told.

Journalists tear themselves away from stories to move on to other issues. In this region every time I practiced the journalistic mantra of detachment, faces from situations like the refugee camps have resurfaced and led me to another compelling situation – each situation worse than the one before. They have challenged my objectivity, my storytelling ability and my journalistic instincts. They gave me an eye for detail and an eye to see the stories from the perspective of the people who were the subjects of my stories.

There is no northeast of India. Like there is no north-west that we know of. Each of these states is unique. Each of the ethnic groups has its own history. To put them into one block is to blur the perspective. And the blur has worked as a divide which deepens every time we categorise events, communities, milestones, achievements in 'stories' from the 'northeast'.

## MANINI **CHATTERJEE**

Manini Chatterjee, 47, is Senior Editor with *The Telegraph.*

**THE AWARD WINNER**
POLITICAL REPORTING, PRINT

# CONGRESS IN THE TIMES OF RAHULJI

WHILE REPORTING ON THE ELECTION CAMPAIGN IN UTTAR PRADESH FOR STATE ASSEMBLY ELECTIONS IN 2007, MANINI CHATTERJEE DISCOVERS INDIA AND WHAT ITS PEOPLE MAKE OF LEADERS LIKE, RAHUL GANDHI AND MAYAWATI.

## CONGRESS IN THE TIMES OF RAHULJI

MUZAFFARNAGAR, KHURJA: PURELY IN TERMS OF A VISUAL experience, the spectacle is guaranteed to warm even the most despairing Congress heart. Men of all ages rush madly to catch a glimpse, women jostle with one another from the balconies of every house that lines the street, and rural boys and urban girls eagerly reach out for a handshake they will talk about for the rest of their lives.

Yes, Rahul Gandhi – interspersing his chopper rides with road shows in kasbas and interior villages of western Uttar Pradesh over the last two days – definitely has star appeal. And if body language is anything to go by, he has certainly come a long way since his first hesitant foray into public life exactly three years ago during the Lok Sabha elections in Uttar Pradesh.

Sitting comfortably atop the carrier of his SUV (Captain Satish Sharma always at the wheel), Rahul reaches out to grasp a hand thrust his way, throw back garlands at the children running alongside, and smile and wave incessantly at the thronging crowds. Mesmerised by the sight of their leader being feted as though he were a sixteenth century Mughal prince or a twenty-first century film star (or both), Congress workers now believe that the party could win around sixty to seventy seats – and all thanks to 'Rahulji'.

But if you stand a little away from the throng, or arrive earlier than Rahul and leave after his chopper has taken off, you soon discover that the reality is not quite as rosy. Sure, Rahul's drawing enthusiastic crowds. But except where the Congress has a strong local contender, his meetings – like a summer shower – leave no lasting impact and are unlikely to change the fortunes of the Congress this time around. And there is no dearth of voices to explain just why.

At Meenakshi Chowk in Muzaffarnagar, a large group of Congress workers, waiting patiently in the sweltering sun for Rahul to arrive, start out insisting that the Congress candidate and former MP Saeeduzaman will win this time. But as the sun gets hotter and the wait begins to get tedious, some of them confess that it's a tough call. Mohammad Taslim, a bystander, makes it clear that the crowds to greet Rahul should not be mistaken for voters. 'He is a famous young man from a famous family. But the fight here is between the SP and the BJP,' he says, adding, 'tell me, why should Muslims vote for the Congress when it does not have any base vote of its own?'

It makes much more sense to vote for SP candidate Chittaranjan Swarup who will get his own caste's vote plus the Muslim vote.

Zaheer Alam, the soft-spoken and erudite qazi of Muzaffarnagar is a veteran Congressman of the old school. But he too admits that although the

Rahul Gandhi: Goodwill yes, but votes?

Congress candidate commands much respect of the community, most Muslims do not want to 'waste' their vote.

In neighbouring Baghra, the Congress has a relatively strong Jat candidate, Pankaj Malik, and in the adjoining Khatauli seat, the Congress is backing Mahendra Singh Tikait's son Rakesh Tikait. As Rahul's chopper lands in Baghra on Sunday evening (from where he embarks on a road show to Tikait's native village Sisouli), we catch up with an old wizened man who is running towards the helipad.

Does he know which leader is arriving, we ask. No, he replies hesitantly, but he knows it is a Congress leader. And who does he plan to vote for? Without thinking for a nanosecond, he replies: 'Mayawati'.

It's an answer that would not surprise old Congressmen in the region. Devendra Singh Thakur, once a prominent local leader in the Muzaffarnagar district, says the best thing the Congress did was not ally with Ajit Singh. 'But Rahul made a big mistake by joining hands with Tikait because the Jats are still the biggest oppressors in this region. Congress has already lost Dalits. It should now focus on the most backward castes. In western Uttar Pradesh, Congress can revive only on the basis of anti-Jat politics,' he insists.

That may be tied to local politics, but the one recurring complaint – whether in the Muzaffarnagar sugarcane belt yesterday or in the towns of Dadri and Khurja where he received a splendid reception today – is that

'*Congress ke paas apna kuch nahin hai*'. (Congress does not have anything of its own.)

Unlike the reigning wisdom in political circles in Delhi which attributes the Congress decline to organisational decay, the more earthy voices we hear blame it on the Congress's outdated 'umbrella' politics. Congress is still caught in the old mould of patronage politics, offering all things to all people, and has been unable to understand – leave alone contend with – the post-Mandal politics of empowerment that has taken its place.

That is why Rahul Gandhi's standard speech – extolling the virtues of the old Uttar Pradesh and bemoaning the 'politics of divisions' over the last fifteen years – is cutting little ice. 'For many people, particularly the Jatavs, things are much better today than they were fifteen years ago. Then they could not even look us in the eye, now we dare not speak against them,' points out Tarseram Gujjar, a businessman in Sikandrabad.

At the end of two days, one thing becomes clear. There is no hostility to the Congress anymore and there is a certain goodwill for 'Indira Gandhi's grandson' in many pockets of Uttar Pradesh.

But neither nostalgia nor charisma are quite enough to change the Congress's fortunes in a polarised polity.

## MAYAWATI: MOVING IN TO FILL THE WESTERN UP VACUUM

BASOLI, UTTAR PRADESH: MAYAWATI MAY NEVER HAVE BEEN to an architecture school nor, as far as we know, taken much interest in Marxist dialectics. But one striking feature of the complex Uttar Pradesh assembly elections of 2007 is the manner in which the Bahujan Samaj Party's 'base-superstructure' experiment is playing itself out in the most unlikely of places. Having built a solid Dalit support base, it is now skilfully trying to erect a multi-hued edifice which, if it succeeds, could recast age-old equations in Uttar Pradesh.

Take this village, for instance. Basoli falls under the Chaprauli assembly segment of Baghpat district in western Uttar Pradesh – the very heart of 'Jatland' which is as associated with Chaudhury Charan Singh as Rae Bareilly-Amethi is with the Gandhis.

Charan Singh's Lok Dal has commanded the loyalty of the dominant Jat community in this entire belt for decades, and Ajit Singh has so far benefited from his father's legacy. Of the fourteen seats the Rashtriya Lok Dal (RLD) won in alliance with the BJP in 2002, eleven came from the Baghpat-Muzaffarnagar region.

But this time, in several of the 'Jat seats', disillusionment with Ajit Singh is palpable. But more significantly, many of them openly state that they will be voting for the BSP. Sanjiv Kumar Tomar, a former deputy pradhan of the village, confesses that the real fight in Chaprauli this time is between the BSP's Gajendra Singh 'Munna' and the RLD's Ajay Tomar – and of the two Jat candidates, Munna has the edge.

'*Yeh pehli baar hai jab Jat bhi haathi par sawar hoga*,' (for the first time the Jat will also ride the elephant), he says. It is a line we hear over and over again not just in Chaprauli but also in Kandhla where the BSP's Jat candidate Balbir Singh has already emerged as the front-runner. Apart from these two seats, BSP has put up a number of Jat candidates throughout this segment of western Uttar Pradesh that goes to the polls in the second phase on 13 April.

That Mayawati has been systematically wooing the Brahmins for the last couple of years is well known. Her decision to give tickets to as many as eighty-six Brahmins is one way of mopping up the votes of the most numerically significant upper caste in Uttar Pradesh.

But in sociological terms, it is the BSP's success in gaining the support (or at least neutralising the hostility) of castes such as the Jats and Banias that is probably more significant. The Congress party's old Brahmin-Dalit equation may have been turned on its head by Mayawati, but the two communities have had a history of cooperation, making it that much easier for the BSP to make inroads into the Brahmin base.

The case of other upper and intermediate castes is very different. The

Jats of western Uttar Pradesh have traditionally suppressed the Dalits in their villages and could not dream of playing second fiddle to the lowest in the social hierarchy. As Ajay Sharma, who runs a shop in Basoli said, 'For all practical purposes, Chaprauli and other seats like it are hundred per cent Jat – the Jats simply do not allow others to vote against their choice.'

But this time it's going to be different. If Jat strongmen like 'Munna' and Balbir Singh get the community's support, they will encourage the Dalits and others to vote since both are now rooting for the BSP. 'Thanks to BSP's clever ticket distribution, it will win more than half the seats in Muzaffarnagar district and come second wherever it does not win,' says Mukesh Pawar Singh in Kandhla.

A similar phenomenon is taking place in many seats outside the Jat belt too. In Ghaziabad town, for instance, the BSP has fielded Suresh Bansal who is putting up a stiff fight against the Congress's Surendra Kumar 'Munni' (who won on an SP ticket last time) and the BJP's Sunil Sharma.

The 'Bania' community which was once solidly behind BJP is now willing to shift its loyalties to the BSP if the party puts up a Bania candidate – as it has done in Ghaziabad, Baghpat and a number of other seats. Anil Kumar, a young trader in Ghaziabad, is not shy of stating why. 'We have always supported BJP. But across UP, only BSP can defeat the Samajwadi Party. In order to end Mulayam's rule, we are voting for the BSP.' Besides, if Mayawati becomes the next CM, 'she might make Bansalji a minister, and then all of us stand to gain,' adds Kumar candidly.

A senior BJP leader from the Jat community who did not wish to be named has a more sophisticated analysis on offer. 'The fact is that in western UP, if not all of UP, only Mayawati has a base vote which is also a transferable vote. Till recently, the Jats were loyal to the Lok Dal and the Banias to the BJP. But that has changed – they are now 'free' castes and will vote for the winning candidate. And the BSP – because of its base vote – has a higher winnability potential in a larger number of seats.'

With the Congress hoping to gain ground after Rahul Gandhi's belated but successful forays in recent weeks, can the BSP's base vote get eroded? Will a section of Dalits return to the Congress's 'umbrella' again?

Ajay Harit, a Dalit student leader at a Ghaziabad college, dismisses the possibility out of hand. '*Jab hamare paas apna ghar nahin tha, hum ashiana dhoondte the. Par apna ghar hone ke baad, hum Congress ke paas kyon jayen?*' (When we did not have our own home, we looked for shelter. But now that we have our own party, why should we go to the Congress?). Ajay Harit's Dalit brethren in the villages may not be quite as articulate but it is thanks to their 'unshakeable' and 'transferable' support that the Jats, Brahmins, Banias and others are thinking of clambering onto the elephant this time.

I WAS TWENTY-THREE YEARS OLD WITH BARELY THREE MONTHS experience in political reporting when I was sent off to cover my first elections in what is arguably the most politicised region of India – eastern Uttar Pradesh. It was the winter of 1984 and the Lok Sabha elections had been called ahead of schedule in the aftermath of Indira Gandhi's tragic assassination. In the Delhi bureau of *The Telegraph* – then a fledgling Calcutta-based daily – I covered the 'opposition' beat. The mood in the Opposition parties, till that horrific morning on 31 October, had been particularly upbeat. Mrs Gandhi, who had made a triumphant comeback in January 1980, had begun to look a lot more vulnerable. Sanjay Gandhi's death had been a shattering personal blow and the Punjab crisis culminating in the bloody Operation Bluestar in June 1984 had taken its toll. The Opposition, though fragmented as always, was confident that alliances and seat adjustments among themselves would once again bring an end to Congress rule.

It might seem amazing in hindsight but even after Mrs Gandhi was assassinated that October morning and Rajiv Gandhi anointed the youngest prime minister of India, Opposition leaders continued to be optimistic. Alliances were unmade and made. Charan Singh's Lok Dal which had formed an alliance with the Bharatiya Janata Party (BJP) under the rubric National Democratic Alliance (NDA) broke off to form a new grouping called Dalit Mazdoor Kisan Party (DMKP). Chandra Shekhar, who had become a hero of sorts for the anti-Congress media after his 1983 *padayatra*, headed another alliance called the United Front. And then there was the newly formed BJP headed by the 'experienced and affable' Atal Behari Vajpayee and the Congress veteran-turned-Indira foe Hemvati Nandan Bahuguna, hopeful of getting the top slot in case of an Opposition victory.

It was in this backdrop that I set off – armed with a bright red portable Brother typewriter that served as both sword and shield – to Allahabad on a cold December morning. For the next three weeks, I crisscrossed – mostly on rickety Uttar Pradesh Road Transport buses – all of eastern Uttar Pradesh. From Allahabad, where the reigning superstar Amitabh Bachchan was pitted against the formidable HN Bahuguna, to Azamgarh where the stylish Chandrajit Yadav (once a 'left' Congressman) was fighting a losing battle against some low-profile Congress candidate. And then north to Gorakhpur and Deoria and Maharajganj (battleground of two famous 'dons' Harishankar Tiwari and LP Shahi); east to Ballia where Chandra Shekhar was surrounded by veteran scribes from Delhi who seemed to regard him as prime minister in waiting; from there to Banaras and then back to Allahabad. And then there was Ghosi and Ghazipur in between – considered the 'red' bastions of Uttar

Pradesh where CPI stalwarts Jharkhande Rai and Sarju Pandey had been living legends for decades.

It was a long journey and I scrupulously followed what I had been told was the election reporter's script. That meant creating as exhaustive a 'constituency profile' as possible. The first stop at any new place was usually the office of the DM (district magistrate) and then the SP (superintendent of police). They provided the 'objective' input – detailed statistics of caste and community (never mind that we haven't had a caste-based census since 1931) and voting patterns over the last few elections. Armed with that information, one went to the local offices of political parties in the fray. I was fascinated with the intricacies of caste equations doled out to me in each constituency. I learnt of the difference between Keoris and Kushwahas; the hostility between Yadavs and Thakurs; the differing voting patterns among various Dalit sub-castes; and how all these factors would play themselves out, each in its own unique way, in different constituencies.

If one had the time, a chat with 'knowledgeable locals' was also in order. The local journalist who gave juicy details about the infighting within a party or the well-placed lawyer or lecturer who explained how a division of votes between two Brahmin candidates of say, the Congress and BJP, would help the Lok Dal's Jat (though this was a Brahmin-dominated seat) pull through.

All this 'background' information, peppered with a quote or two from that ubiquitous taxi driver, would be leavened with 'field reporting' – i.e. colour copies on political rallies and speeches. Amitabh's baritone dialogue delivery coupled with Jaya Bhaduri's attempt to woo voters with her *Guddi* smile provided enough verbiage for a couple of Page One anchors as did a day-long travel through backward Ballia in Chandra Shekhar's convoy. The battle between the dons in Maharajganj and young workers cycling through Ghosi with red flags fluttering atop the handlebars made for some interesting stories. As for predictions, I stuck to the tried and tested 'neck and neck fight' and 'silent voter' images that are among the easiest ways to cover an election without actually saying anything.

And after three weeks of being in the field, I am ashamed to say that I got the landmark 1984 elections wrong. Okay, I was more or less certain that Amitabh would win and realised that Chandra Shekhar may be a media hero, but he was just a 'Thakur' leader in Ballia. But as far as the big picture goes, I got it terribly wrong. Even today I cringe when I recall the headline of one of my reports (mercifully buried inside the newspaper) – 'No sympathy wave, caste factor crucial'.

In retrospect, I am glad of that blunder. For it taught me two cardinal lessons about election reporting that have helped me enormously over the last two decades in covering umpteen elections – and getting most of them more or less right.

The first, and by far the most important lesson I learnt is that elections are about people. That might seem a very obvious, even trite, conclusion for aren't we forever boasting about India being the world's largest democracy? And it is the world's largest only because we are the second most populous nation on earth and China is a one-party state.

But after covering election after election in different parts of the country, I would argue that India is a great democracy not just because of the numbers but because of the involvement of the people – ordinary, faceless, voiceless citizens who count for nothing except on polling day – in the electoral process. Elections are the lifeblood of our democracy and some election or the other – panchayat, municipal corporation, Assembly or Lok Sabha – is taking place in some part or another of the country around the year.

And no matter how rich or powerful a politician may be, he has to return to the people again and again to seek a mandate. And despite the cynicism of the middle classes towards politicians, the vast mass of ordinary Indians take elections seriously because it is the only time when they are wooed and sought after; the one – possibly the only – time when all Indians are equal because each adult male or female has that one crucial vote.

It has become something of a cliché to say that the two abiding passions of the Indian people as a whole are cricket and cinema. But any reporter who has travelled to the countryside at election time would realise that there is a third passion – and that is politics. And unlike cricket or the movies, elections are not a spectator sport but a participatory exercise of unparalleled dimensions.

This is something we often forget. Political reporting usually focuses on political leaders and occasionally on political processes just as sports reporting deals with sportsmen and their game and business reporting with business tycoons and corporate policy. But politics is different. The politician is important only in so far as he represents a large number of people. Between elections, these people may cease to matter but at election time, it is they who take centrestage.

The mistake I made in 1984 (and which remains the 'standard' method of election reporting even today) was to depend on the 'people who matter' – candidates and political leaders, local intelligentsia, Delhi-based 'experts' and poll pundits. This is not to say that these inputs are useless. It is good to read up on a constituency, meet local leaders, attend political rallies and lend half an ear to opinion-makers in the national and state capitals who claim to have a finger on the pulse of the people. But at the end of the day the only way to gauge the mood of the people is to talk to the voters themselves. There is only one thing more important than that – to listen to them.

The Indian voter is a shrewd customer regardless of his or her levels of education or wealth. In fact, it is a universal phenomenon that the level of disinterest in politics increases as one goes up the socio-economic ladder. It has been my experience over and over again – be it in Uttar Pradesh or Bihar or Himachal Pradesh or Gujarat or Chhattisgarh – that the so-called 'humble' and 'unlettered' voter remains deeply involved with the democratic process and often is more knowledgeable and insightful on political issues than our own tribe of political commentators and journalists who are held up as pundits.

I am always wonderstruck when a marginal farmer or a car mechanic or (though less common) a village woman can reel out the names of all the candidates and their political affiliations each time one stops at a wayside chai shop or enters a village bylane, and give a succinct account of the main issues in the battle.

Drawing them out is not easy. Over the years, I have learnt what to ask and more important what not to ask. Never ask a voter who he or she is backing. In rare cases, when several people spread across a constituency are forthcoming with their views without any prompting it is a sure indication that of a 'wave' in the making. But for the most part, no one likes to reveal to a rank stranger at the outset of a conversation his or her voting preference. In the beginning, they often tell you 'God only knows who will win' or direct you to the local bigwig for answers.

It is only when they realise that the reporter is genuinely interested in listening to them and when the reporter does not talk down to them that the 'ordinary' voter opens out. On a road journey through a constituency, I try and stop at least a dozen times. Sometimes a conversation in a teashop somewhere in the boondocks can last for hours with everyone pitching in and supporters of rival parties nearly coming to blows. And then there are times when only one or two people will speak and not say much. After numerous such conversations, one begins to see a pattern. Of course, a reporter can never cover as much ground or talk to as many people as opinion pollsters and their market research teams claim to do. But reporters usually get a better picture than a pollster because of the nature of questions and answers. A chance remark can reveal the electoral mood better than reams of questionnaires; a pithy comment can sum up a complex political process far more effectively than any ponderous political commentary.

In the Bihar assembly elections in February 2005, for instance, Lalu Prasad Yadav was supremely confident of victory as usual. Dismissing the threat posed by a fractured opposition, Lalu told us in his inimitable style, '*Is ghich pich mein lalten hi jalta rahega*' (in this confusion, the lantern – the RJD election symbol – will shine). I heard many speeches by Ram Vilas Paswan and Sushil Modi and Nitish Kumar attacking Lalu but I knew the RJD supremo was in trouble only after meeting a young villager, Ram Pukar Yadav, in an out-of-the-way hamlet called Sagarpur in Madhubani district of north Bihar. Ram Pukar did not give any lengthy sermon. Sitting atop a buffalo, his laconic reply on the RJD's prospects was: '*Jab mitti ka tel tees rupaiyya litre hai, to lalten kaise jalayenge?*' (When kerosene costs Rs 30 per litre, how do you expect us to light the lantern?)

It was much the same in Uttar Pradesh in the summer of 2007. Voices from the ground gave enough indication of a BSP surge even though pollsters were hedging their bets about how badly the Assembly would be hung. In a village in the Jat heartland of western Uttar Pradesh, Mayawati's tactic of giving BSP tickets to powerful local Jats (a caste known for its hostility to Dalits) was clearly working. '*Yeh pehli baar hai jab Jat bhi haathi par sawar hoga*' ( this is the first time that Jats will ride the elephant) was a comment we heard more than once till it became something of a refrain.

That the BSP's 'social engineering' formula of bringing Dalits and Brahmins on the same platform wasn't some learned thesis was brought home to us in Hastpur village near Mathura where an unlettered Brahmin woman, Radha Rani, explained in her rustic dialect the winning formula of the sitting BSP MLA Mukul Upadhyaya. '*Jatav log haathi par vote denge, hum Mukul bhai ko,*' (the Dalits will vote for the symbol, we will vote for the candidate).

In Uttar Pradesh and Bihar almost everyone breathes politics and entire afternoons can be spent listening to arguments and analyses in a village square shop beneath the shade of a peepul tree. But if one is patient and curious, there are gems to come by in every part of the country.

I remember a drive through the picturesque Konkan coast in Maharashtra during the Assembly elections of 2004. Konkan had long served as the Shiv Sena bastion but Narayan Rane's departure had put a question mark on the Sena's fortunes. Long before I reached Chiplun in Ratnagiri district, I knew the Sena was in trouble from the stray comments I gathered en route. '*Chiplun mein bahut tough hain*', I was told. And the main reason was the Sena had denied a ticket to the sitting MLA and given it to an 'outsider' called Prabhakar Shinde. Or as a shopkeeper put it drily, '*Shinde to Bambai se parcel hain, Chiplun main koi nahin pehchanta usko.*' (Shinde is a parcel from Mumbai, in Chiplun no one knows him.) I reached Chiplun late, did not go to any party office or rally and was worried that I may have relied too much on an apolitical shopkeeper in another constituency. But he proved to be right – the Sena lost the seat by a big margin.

And in Gujarat in December 2007, I knew that Modi was on his way back when a former Congress supporter told me, 'The Congress is a bunch of eunuchs. Indira Gandhi was a real leader. Today Modi is our Indira Gandhi.' Later, when large numbers of Muslims in the old city of Ahmedabad said they were reconciled to another spell of BJP rule, I knew I had lost my bet in Delhi because the ground reality in Gujarat told a different story.

And that brings me to the second lesson I learnt back in 1984 – never let your political biases come in the way of your election reporting. That is not always easy because considering the massive size of the electorate even in an Assembly constituency, you will always find enough voices to support the party/candidate you would like to see win. It is essential, then, to talk to a wide cross section and at the end of the day sift through your notes to get an idea of which way the wind may be blowing. Unless it is a very close election, there is usually a discernible tilt one way or another and one can predict the trend (which is what we are meant to do rather than come out with specific numbers). The first requirement in being objective is to acknowledge one's subjectivities. As political beings, we all have our ideological preferences and antipathies. Once one acknowledges, at least to oneself, this subjective bias, it is a lot easier to combat it in the field and go out of one's way to listen to people who speak a different language. In Gujarat, for instance, I was hoping that Narendra Modi would lose. Before going there, I was convinced that in a 'normal' election, the people would vote out a sectarian agenda. But after a week in Gujarat I realised that Modi had packaged himself as a development hero and Hindutva had become a lot more subliminal than in 2002. Similarly, in 1991 it was clear that even the non-upper castes of Uttar Pradesh had been caught in the frenzy of the Ramjanmabhoomi movement and were rooting for the BJP – something most of my secular tribe refused to see. But the job of the reporter is to convey the atmosphere and the dynamics of the situation on the ground, even if it goes against one's own political preferences and hopes. There is also the fear of getting an election wrong or writing something that would invoke the wrath or abuse of one's ideological soulmates back home. It is difficult but necessary to ignore these fears if one wants to do an honest job of election reporting.

Elections, in the end, are not the most important part of election reporting. As far as I am concerned, elections are only an excuse and an opportunity for a reporter to have the time of her life. For the most part, newspapers only report about people who matter and reporters only go to the 'spot' when something untoward takes place – a riot or a natural disaster. But at election time, you can travel freely through the countryside, enter any village, talk to anyone and listen to voices you never otherwise pay attention to. Elections are the best time to discover India and no matter how many elections you cover, there is always a fresh discovery. For me, they have been a constant reaffirmation of the innate civility and wisdom of India's 'ordinary people' and their extraordinary role in the making of our democracy.

MAYANK **SHEKHAR**

Mayank Shekhar, 28, is freelance film critic and columnist. He is also a popular face on television presenting film reviews.

**THE AWARD WINNER**
FILMS AND TELEVISION, PRINT

# WHERE NO ONE'S A NAMESAKE

IN THIS REVIEW OF A FILM BASED ON JHUMPA LAHIRI'S NOVEL, *THE NAMESAKE*, SHEKHAR, FINDS IN THE STORY OF MIGRATION, THE STORY OF HUMAN PROGRESS.

'BEING A FOREIGNER,' ASHIMA, THE PROTAGONIST OF JHUMPA Lahiri's *The Namesake* describes, 'is a sort of lifelong responsibility – a perpetual wait, a constant burden, a continuous feeling out of sorts. It is an ongoing responsibility, a parenthesis in what had once been ordinary life, replaced by something more complicated and demanding.' It is much simpler to stay forever where you call home; among people and processes you choose and set for yourself.

Ashima is a quiet girl, perhaps in her late teens, in a crowded, cozy Calcutta family. Her move to the anonymous West in the late 70s is an outcome of marriage. On the wedding night, in Mira Nair's deeply felt adaptation of Lahiri's novel, Ashima's grandmother gently holds her hand and whispers that while 'she must embrace the new, she mustn't forget the old'. It may not be as stoically easy to do both, she realises soon.

A great film, like a great restaurant, expends more energy, resources and thought than may befit the first cursorily savoured moments of joy. It requires going back to. I did this time to sample *The Namesake*, less for its sweepingly generic vignettes from thirty-plus years of a 300-page novel, but to focus instead on the personal. Of course, I felt mildly moist-eyed over two scenes: when both Ashima and her son Gogol lose their parent. It's too evocative and manipulated a moment to remain untouched by. But Nair's film, to me, seemed more lucidly a fair meditation on the first-generation migrant, his complicated relation with home, of both origin and adoption: a delicately imperfect balance between separation and integration that is, by turns, a burden and a responsibility.

Ashoke Ganguly could be a labourer from Bihar, returning from the city, with dark 'Roy-Ben' goggles in his eyes, two-in-one stereo system on his shoulder, and stories to regale the awed village of a world they've never known. I don't know if it's still the same. The loved, affable 'Non-Resident Indian' uncles and cousins (every home had one; bankers, engineers, et al) of my years growing up were no different: a holy cross between Santa Claus and a superstar, they got back gifts from a good life we flaunted in our neighbourhood; drank bottled water we found too sanitised for taste; and their curiously pampered children often whined in an accent we made it our duty to comprehend. I occasionally envied them, but waited more for their late-night return (and the Nintendo game, or at least the 6-feet bubble gum). The scene gets repeated as the excited, joint Ganguly family welcomes Ashoke, Ashima and their children in a reception that's no less than a community feast. The observed affection and energy of this homecoming is discernible.

Tabu and Irfan Khan in a still from *The Namesake*

Migration is the story of human progress; a close, warm and accepting family is the pain it leaves behind. It may be easier to be a travelling salesman if the said immediate roots we confuse for culture or tradition are not as deep-seated.

We find an anonymous Ashima in Boston or New York, once always surrounded by relatives, now grappling with the loneliness of a walk to the laundromat on a snowy day, the couple attempting to find sameness among other Bengali families, the loss of perhaps a large, known cultural space. They are perhaps more Bengali than many in Bengal, though American to those back home. They know their reasons for existence: a life of opportunities for their children.

The conflict over identity is really their son Gogol's. He appears limited by it: a reason American Born Confused Desi (ABCD or its British variant) may soon be a word in the English dictionary (if it already isn't); a recognisable inferiority complex you could observe even among second-generation migrants from villages and small-towns into big cities in India.

We're all migrants at some level. The liberating moment is when we treat sacrifices and heritage of a previous generation as a rich identity.

THERE'S AN OBSERVATION OF RURAL NORTH INDIAN STREET-speak that goes, '*Gareeb ki joru; sabki bhabi*!' In a rough English translation this suggests that in a *basti*, people suppose a poor man's wife to be their sister-in-law. They certainly call her that: '*bhabiji*'; – '*Aur kya chal raha hai, bhabiji?* (How're things?)', '*Kahaan jaa rahin hain, bhabiji?* (Where're you going?)', '*Kaisi hain, bhabiji?* (How are you?).'

Well, I don't know about her, but I don't always feel that great.

It isn't so hard to develop expertise on certain subjects. Opinion of any kind is relatively easy to pass off as such. Everyone follows films in India, even if they don't watch that many of them. What does it take to assume a view on such a phenomenon? Nearly, nothing. The chattering aunty next-door can gossip all day, she may as well write about films; same difference! You will take her seriously, in the same way you won't if she made a persuasive point about politics.

Correspondingly, Bollywood pretty much becomes that '*bhabi*' among writers (or journalists) in this country. Even among serious-minded social observers, it is frequently the reference point for popular psychology, and metaphor for as many communal theories. This may not be such a bad thing. Generalisations as they may be, the analogies often work. The box-office is a polling booth where a good proportion of India goes in together to vote every week. Often, a lot can be made of how a community thinks from what it enjoys, and collectively responds to.

It's only worrying sometimes for a genre of journalism when there are twice the numbers of quick commentators (under the guise of dedicated reviewers) of films each week as there are of films made annually. If that numeric fact appears tame, remember, we still make the most movies in the world.

One of cinema's most unusual critiques, I am told, was for a 1941 American film called *You're In the Army Now*. That film is also credited in the Guinness Book for the most number of kisses on screen. The reviewer was apparently unimpressed. He (or she) merely said, 'Absolutely disgusting!' Strong piece of caution up there for sure, but there is no narrative appeal to this supposed piece; and of course no writing at all – just, 'absolutely disgusting'. While that should count for opinion, I am not certain if it makes for a review.

It isn't enough to suggest that something doesn't (or does) work for you. It is important to search inward (or outward) and explain why; in a way that hopefully someone else always cannot. Those thoughts and insights and arguments and points and world-view constitute a review. Unfortunately, what largely appears on the Indian media does not make that definition.

The jockey on the radio goes, 'A must-watch'. The lady in the morning daily mentions, 'mandatory viewing', almost every other weekend. The television anchor makes a similar noise on his television show. So does the chap on a popular website. The half-baked, arrogant sanction of approval (or disapproval), is followed by the film's intimately detailed story line; actor A's brilliant, actor B not so, actor C so-so; cinematography par excellence; but the film is too long … A few more clichés, a few puns, yet some more superlatives, or equally strong criticism, if you haven't liked a work as much.

The above observations essentially qualify for a film review. Any reviewer can derive legitimacy from a film's cover that carries his one-line reco, over the name of a website, newspaper, television or radio station he offers opinion through. The picture, in turn, gains critical mileage. Its posters progressively gather more names and blurbs, over weeks. By the first weekday in any case, it's time to announce the film a 'super hit'. This ever-growing drill is an effective, though by now a fairly predictable, part of a publicity-industrial design.

The public will not know one opinion-maker from the other. Unfortunately, critics are always known as a collective, never quite referred to (or thought of) as individuals. The reader (or listener or viewer) follows advice, assuming unanimous acclaim. None of it may have anything to do with reviews, or writing or reflection in general. But such is roughly the state of film criticism in India, at once devalued by the industry that makes films (which isn't any of my business), and the infotainment media (which is) that increasingly feeds on it – both grossly indifferent toward intellect and integrity in general.

It helps the devils of non-fiction that there is no profession in this country known as film criticism either. Many reviewers, given their inclination towards the film medium, naturally harbour ambitions to take up screenwriting or feature-film direction themselves. This may be a one-time movement in a career. In certain film cultures, it is seen as an organic progression for an established critic as well.

Several revered films, right from John Houston's *Fort Apache* or John Ford's *The African Queen* in the 40s and 50s, down to Mike Newell's *Donnie Brasco* or Martin Scorsese's *Gangs Of New York* in the 90s and 2000s were written (or co-written) by those who were once resident film critics with major publications (like *The New York Times, Washington Post, Newsweek* or *Time*). The examples are too many. There is then the French New Wave cinema of the 60s, started out entirely by directors who were first film critics with *Cahiers du Cinema*: Goddard, Truffaut, Jacques Rivette, Eric Rohmer, and Claude Chabrol. LK Advani was at one point, a movie critic. Yet the *New Yorker* giant Pauline Kael, arguably the greatest exponent of the art of film criticism, never made a film.

There is in fact little direct association between film-criticism and filmmaking; the first is an entirely deconstructive process, just as the second is a constructive one. The critic doesn't tell the filmmaker what she should not have done. He merely tells his readers what she has. A great film critic need not make an equally good director. The reverse is equally true. The argument that those who cannot create, critique instead, is an unfair one. Criticism is an act of creation in itself. It is rarely seen as such.

There is then the other side, where most reviewers in general are also trade magazine publishers or entertainment editors or gossip writers or reporters on the lifestyle and celebrity beat, or hosts and anchors for media companies. A few even double up as self-appointed or official public relation professionals.

You can sense the uneasy distance between the film critic and the film industry itself. This relationship can be relatively symbiotic or incestuous, depending on your preferred usage. If there is no full-time occupation called film criticism to begin with, you're unlikely to take as seriously the responsibilities that come with the said job: most of all, uninhibited honesty. A film review which isn't worth much in terms of money, has the reputation of a film worth millions of bucks riding on it. The criticism at the same time carries with it the trust of a million readers. It can become difficult, sometimes, to see clearly, whose side you're really on.

Within all this, the public may be tempted to question who the thought-leaders of pop culture are, and why their opinions should be taken seriously when they are quite obviously unconvincing (perhaps for reasons of a writer's persuasive skills), or uninformed (because just about anyone with an opinion is a critic), or even unscrupulous (for dishonesties both moral and monetary, regularly associated with reviewers)?

As it turns out, the public hardly questions. Most don't read reviews. They merely take a glance at 'star ratings' – that perversely reductive curse handed down to film criticism. Most criticisms of reviewers are also essentially centred on this brainless premise: how come he gave those films two stars; that one three; and the other one four. (Come on, the third one wasn't twice as good as the first; the two with the same ratings weren't the same in quality either ...). As if reviews were an algorithm and not a lively debate; and the final rating, some definitive mathematical solution. I'm afraid, the rate at which the space for reviews in mainline papers in the West has begun to shrink, what we may be left with is merely a few silly emotions and a tiny comment.

There is no need to entirely pass on the blame to the unknown reader. I am not particularly proud of my own tribe (while it only keeps growing by the day). Rarely do I publicly admit my profession, rightly held to be low-brow enough to give entry-level, call-centre executives an intellectual superiority complex. If films are silly (Hindi films are largely known to be), it is supposed that the job of reviewing them should be sillier still. The word 'filmy' will remain a common Indian pejorative for years, even as we speak now of an urban renaissance in Mumbai films.

Most Hindi movies do not merit comment beyond the oddly funny descriptions of their preposterous premises. It is true. But so is the popular 'Sturgeon's Law': 90 per cent of everything is crud. Yet, it gets widely consumed.

With films, for instance, and this applies as much to junk food, pulp literature, street fashion, etc., the quality of a work can be inversely proportional to its appeal (in some cases, I feel, it necessarily is). Appreciation for the sort of cinema where entertainment isn't the only purpose (though it will always remain the primary one) isn't a simple matter of class either. You could meet a taxi driver, who given the exposure, loves a *Kaagaz Ke Phool,* a H*azaaron Khwaishein Aisi* or *Swades*, and is a fan of Ray, Benegal or at least Mani Ratnam.

Likewise, I'm sure you've noticed, most educated people (some of them doctors, engineers, professors, collegians), when it comes to their taste in films, would much rather watch David Dhawan's thirty-eighth rehashed comedy. Whenever asked by friends to recommend a film for them, I'm almost always asked for something 'light' (a word that isn't easy to explain in this context). Some of these readers of reviews are the least fond of critics. They find them pompously instructional; cultural snobs or cynics or kill-joys; intellectually disconnected with the masses the movies are made for.

I think you will hate a lot of films, and express it, only when you love films as much. In just the same way, you will be critical of the nation you choose to live in, only if you loved it enough to bother. There can be no other agenda. To repeatedly suggest your country (or its people or its government) sucks, is a more comfortable notion of patriotism than, 'no *roti* (bread), no *kapda* (clothes), no *makaan* (homes); but *mera bharat mahaan* (my country is great)'. On occasions that the nation appears great (and it does), you're then as passionate in your praise as you've been aggressive in criticism. I digress only a little bit. To politicians (like it is to filmmakers), an honest, unbiased voice is the only thing that comes between their audience and the advertisement. They'd much rather it entirely disappeared; unless, it was part of the advertisement.

I'm often told that if one were to go by my reviews every weekend, nobody would watch too many films in the first place. That I take films too seriously. I do, because I humbly care. This doesn't quite mean that I take myself as seriously. I don't think it is my job to tell readers whether they will like a film or not. It may be natural to assume so, especially in the mainstream press. There are hundreds of films made in a year (a good portion of them in Mumbai). Nobody can possibly watch everything. The viewer needs somebody to help them decide.

It is but hugely condescending to assume anybody's opinion (even 'God's') to be the truth. Only marketers think that way. Like all art, criticism is personal to the point of being autobiographical. The reviewer walks in to a picture, observes a world from a distance, attempts to absorb what's before him, and finally returns with a readable commentary that reveals as much about the reviewer as it does about the film. This is no different from any of the writing lately being termed 'creative non-fiction': travelogue, reportage, pop-history, etc. Film criticism in India, however, never gets that sort of respect. It is merely reduced to a '*thenga dekhai*' (show your thumb): if it's up, you're doomed; doomed you are, if it's down.

If you loved a work and so did everyone later on, the observation is considered obvious, the work great. Eventually, after weeks of relentless hype, the film by many is deemed over-rated, and the reviewer gone overboard. It's the same the other way. Nobody acknowledges that the critic watches a film before anyone else. He is nervously alone with his thoughts then, knowing he'll be judged the next morning, unaware how millions may (or may not) react to the film thereafter. As many readers love a review as they hate them. This is expected of any subjective opinion.

Also, a director or lead actor (or anybody associated with a film) is unlikely to think too highly of your critique when you haven't thought quite highly of their creativity; it's natural. Unfortunately, in Mumbai, you are never too far from where they live; you frequent the same public places they do; at times you even share a common social circle. I recognised quite early on in my career never to make friends in the films, because losing them was a certainty.

The reader won't always bat for your honesty; neither will the movie industry, unless you're already sold to their team. This is a thankless job from both ends: little respect, no money, and hardly any personal influence (when you're perceived as a collective to begin with). Why do I do it, if I know that's true? The first obvious confession is I love watching movies more than most other things: the worst of them are amusing; the best can change your life forever.

The second is, funny as that may sound, I find writing about films could be a fair foil to articulate pop intellectualism. *Forbes* did a survey in 2007 on who America thought were its top pundits, or leading opinion-makers. On its top-ten list were of course the expected, popular commentators of varied political persuasions, the Bill O'Reilly, Rosie O'Donnell and Geraldo Rivera. At No. 2, to the surprise of many, was a loved, libertarian stand-up comedian Bill Maher.

The No. 1 name that the poll revealed, however, was a gentleman called Roger Ebert. He writes film reviews that read like personal accounts on television, and in the *Chicago Sun Times*. I admire his writing. I was not particularly shocked, only happy. Ebert is also the only film critic to receive the Pulitzer Prize.

A film review quite subtly allows you the breadth to push forward a personal world-view: on politics, sex, current events, social phenomena, anything. It isn't always easy, but there's scope. There are definitely more eyes on that film column than there are on intense editorials on the same subject. Cinema can concern itself with any part of our lives. So can its commentary. Once the reader is sufficiently warmed up into picking up the piece first, there is chance he and the writer would begin to think together, share values and thoughts and opinions, and not about the said film alone.

What do they know of films, if films are all they know? It is great, perhaps, to hang out with the *bhabi* more, if you wish to get through to Ramesh!

## NILANJANA **BOSE**

Nilanjana Bose, 30, is Senior Special Correspondent with CNN-IBN.

**THE AWARD WINNER**
UNCOVERING INDIA INVISIBLE, BROADCAST

# LIVING POSITIVE

WHAT CAN A FUTURE HOLD FOR CHILDREN WHO HAVE LOST THEIR PARENTS TO HIV-AIDS? NILANJANA BOSE TRAVELS TO GUNTUR DISTRICT IN ANDHRA PRADESH AND MEETS THESE LITTLE ADULTS.

WHEN I SET OFF FOR HYDERABAD FROM DELHI, I WAS prepared for what I was going to see in Andhra Pradesh's Guntur district. Little orphans who had suddenly stepped into adult shoes. I knew what their faces would be like. I had already in my mind, painted pictures of children with pain in their eyes and hunger in their bellies. I had met such children before – children who had grown up before they were meant to. So I knew what to expect. Or so I thought.

When I met Rekha at her workplace – the field where she worked as an agricultural labourer – in Upalpadu village, I realised this child did not fit the stereotype I had conjured in my mind. I was to realise later, that the story was going to be the same with every HIV-AIDS orphan I was to meet later on that trip. Rekha was seventeen – a tall, strapping girl, brimming with self-confidence and a shy smile that never left her face. Even as I tried to find the words to tell her why I wanted to tell the story of her life, she said, without a trace of grief: 'I am an orphan – I lost my parents to HIV-AIDS, I have given up going to school and I support my little siblings. And there are dozens like me in this village and in the entire state.' And, she emphasised, 'There is nothing strange about being an HIV-AIDS orphan. It's a part of life for children here, a responsibility we take on, without batting an eyelid.'

For me, that was the moment when I realised that this story would have to be told differently. My carefully prepared storyboard found its place in the dustbin. And I decided to let the children tell their own stories instead of me acting as narrator. In television it's always a gamble to use a format like this – to let your case studies act as the *sutradhar*. But the children I met in Guntur and Vijaywada were not only eloquent but their stories were such that they could only be told by those who had lived them.

In the two weeks that I spent there, I would often find myself crossing that fine line between being a journalist and a human being moved by a story. The lives of Rekha, Senthil and Laxmi were such that there were moments when I wondered how they could go about their lives in a normal manner pretending they were just like any one else. But I now realise that it was that very belief that got them through each day of their lives. Each child would wear an armour that would protect him or her from snide comments or taunting remarks. Yes, they were HIV-AIDS orphans. Their parents were dead and they could be infected themselves. It was not a hypothetical situation. It was a way of life for them. It didn't matter how young they were when fate dealt them an ugly blow. A little child I met in Guntur was left with just an ageing grandmother – a retired sex worker with a broken leg who was also diagnosed with HIV-AIDS. The child, Pushpa, had recently been diagnosed with the same. As one of the neighbours put it: 'No one knew who would go first, the grandmother or the grandchild.'

They were so used to being treated as outcasts, that sometimes the smallest of gestures would make these little adults become the children that they actually were – their eyes brimming with tears. I remember shooting in Vijaywada with twelve-year-old Laxmi, when it suddenly started to rain. In what seemed like a natural thing to do, I pulled Laxmi under an umbrella and started walking with my arm around her shoulder. When we finally found a shelter, I realised she had tears in her eyes. She later told our translator that very few people touched her because people thought they would get infected with HIV-AIDS if they did.

'Living Positive' was in many ways, a gamble that paid off. Not only did we practically allow the children to decide what kind of form the documentary would take, but we also did something that unfortunately, very few television channels do: protect the identities of such children.

I had already decided before we landed in Andhra Pradesh that we would shoot the film in such a way that their faces wouldn't be identifiable. In television, there's a very simple way of doing this: mosaicing (the fuzzy layer that often comes over the face of a rape victim for example). But we decided that 'Living Positive' would have none of that because the pictures look doctored. So we agreed to put in an extra bit of effort – shoot all the sequences with the children, against light. In other words, we would film the children standing or sitting with their faces against light (tube lights, bulbs, sunlight) rather than facing it. As a result, their faces are dark, rather than lit up. However, as simple as that sounds, it's not the easiest thing to pull off in television. It's an extremely painstaking and time-consuming process where every shot has to be framed carefully and executed perfectly. Changing their names and dubbing their voices were the other precautions we took – so that the children wouldn't be recognised after the story went on air.

At some point of time during shooting 'Living Positive', I almost took Rekha and the other children for granted. I believed they were children made of Teflon who could feel no pain. I thought being strong came naturally to them. Rekha and I bonded as two women. We were years apart but she treated me like I was a seventeen-year-old like her. One day while sharing a cup of tea she suddenly started talking about marriage and children. So I started pulling her leg and asked her whether she fancied any one. My questions were met with a stony silence. I thought, maybe I had crossed some invisible line so I immediately shut up. After a few moments of uncomfortable silence she looked at me and asked: 'Do you think any one would want to marry me? Do you think I have the right to think about marriage when I have to raise my younger siblings and take care of them?'

It was during moments like this that I realised the cross she had been carrying after her parents passed away leaving behind in her care, the unfortunate legacy of HIV-AIDS. The truth was that children like Rekha had no future. And even while I told her otherwise, I knew she was old enough to understand that hers was a life that needed courage to live. And I often wondered how many people were capable of such courage.

For that matter, even some of the adults lived with a kind of courage that no parent wants to.

When we met little Kumar in a small village in Guntur, I couldn't help but wonder at how cruel life can be sometimes for him and his recently divorced mother. When the little boy had fallen ill, the doctor had suggested a blood transfusion. Since his father's blood group was the same as Kumar's, the father decided to give him blood. What no one knew was that he was HIV positive. Within months, Kumar tested positive himself. Scorned by his friends at school, Kumar's mother decided to let the boy stay at home. A few months after we returned from Guntur, I was told he was seriously ill and didn't have much of a chance to survive. I have to admit I didn't call after that to check how he was. A part of me was scared to.

From villages with little child-adults to one of the biggest red-light areas down South – Chilakaluripet – HIV-AIDS seemed to have spread its tentacles all over Andhra Pradesh. While sharing a cup of tea with a sex worker, I was told rather candidly: if the customer says I will pay you Rs 1,000 instead of Rs 300 for one night without using a condom, what is the smart thing to do? Especially when you have four mouths to feed at home? It was a toss-up between smart economics and health. But this young woman had her priorities in place. And since most women thought on similar lines, I met dozens of women who had been infected. And those who continued to work, following the same mantra of no condom if the client paid double or triple. When I tried to explain to them the ramifications of something like this, I was greeted with a sarcastic laugh and a few angry words in Telugu. Going by the shocked expression on my translator's face, I have a fair idea what those words meant.

For the longest time I couldn't understand how most of the people I met there – whose lives had been affected directly or indirectly by HIV-AIDS – seemed so blasé. That is when I realised that they all had a very fatalistic approach to life. They believed that life and death were not in their hands. It was not some thing they could control. So they just lived each day as it presented itself. Every time I tried to convince Rekha, Laxmi and the other children to get tested, they would laugh it off. Laxmi told me she didn't want to know. 'I have one life to live,' she told me. 'I want to live this life without fear. If I discover I'm positive, I'll fail in my responsibilities towards my siblings.'

Towards the end of my stay there I desperately needed to look for some thing positive out of everything I had witnessed there. Try as I did, I couldn't find any semblance of hope in the lives that these children were leading. Sitting in the village playground watching dozens of little children play, I would wonder how many of them were infected with HIV-AIDS. A local health worker who was helping us in Guntur had told me earlier that the villages we visited had several children who had tested positive. And then of course, there were so many who hadn't even been tested. Left on their own, shunned by their neighbours, theirs was a life that few would want in exchange.

As journalists we always strive to be detached from the stories we cover, so that we can be objective in our reportage. But sometimes there are assignments where you can't help but get pulled along into a whirlpool of emotions. Before I returned to Delhi, I knew I just had to find something positive – something with a ray of hope.

That hope came in the form of Venkat Rao and his wife Parvati – who lived in a slum in Vijaywada. The couple had four sons but that didn't stop them from adopting Nageshwar – their neighbour's son. Nagesh's parents had both died of HIV-AIDS. And before thinking how they would manage to raise another son on their joint monthly income of Rs 5,000, they adopted the ten year-old orphan. I remember spending a day with the Raos while shooting with them for the documentary. There was no question of how much he meant to his new parents. Even when the cameras were not rolling, Parvati couldn't take her protective eyes off her eldest son. For me, that was the hope I needed to close the shoot of 'Living Positive'.

After the programme went on air, there were many calls from viewers. Some were appalled, a lot of them distressed by what they saw. Several people offered to help the children – to put them through school and to pay them money. I am not sure if those offers were taken up by the children. Knowing them, I don't think they would have wanted to go back to school. And no amount of money would have given their lost lives and parents back to them.

Assignments are, at the end of the day, assignments, stories we cover and report for our viewers. It's usually just another day. Very few assignments actually impact us and make us stop and think. To imagine that something like HIV-AIDS can render so many children orphans and that there are such few interventions in place in India to take care of them – is something that is unfathomable. At the end of the day, as journalists we are just storytellers. We tell a story as best as we can, in the hope that somewhere we have been able to make a difference in the lives of the characters of the story. 'Living Positive' was my little contribution to the memory of the hundreds of lives that have been lost – and the thousand more lives that are being lost. Still.

RAJDEEP **SARDESAI**

One of the most popular faces on television, Rajdeep Sardesai, 43, is Editor-in-Chief CNN-IBN.

**THE AWARD WINNER**
JOURNALIST OF THE YEAR, BROADCAST

## JOURNALISM OF COURAGE

IN A RARE ACCOUNT OF HIS LIFE AS A JOURNALIST, RAJDEEP SARDESAI GOES DOWN MEMORY LANE AND WRITES ABOUT HIS EXPERIENCES AND COMMITMENT TO HIS CHOSEN PROFESSION.

ONE OF THE ENDURING CHARMS OF JOURNALISM IS THAT NO two days are the same. On 13 December 2001, I was engaging in light banter with my cameraperson near Parliament. For most MPs, Fridays mark the beginning of a long weekend: private member bills are discussed and extended lunches are planned. My cameraperson suggested: 'Boss, nothing is happening in Parliament today, *chutti ka mahaul hai* (it's a holiday atmosphere). Let's go to Andhra Bhavan for lunch. I will then go home to sleep.' Fifteen minutes later, any thought of a siesta was consigned to a distant dream, lunch at Andhra Bhavan remained an unfulfilled desire. A little after 11.30 am, television screens were buzzing, for once with genuine breaking news: India's Parliament had been attacked by terrorists.

Much of journalism is pure luck: we were incredibly fortunate to find ourselves bang in the middle of one of the biggest stories of our times. For almost the next twenty-four hours, we were literally on air, on the move, documenting each and every moment of a dramatic day in the life of the Indian nation. The news adrenalin was flowing: for a journalist, it's a magic potion, one that can recharge the body and soul like little else.

Most right-thinking citizens dread riots, terror attacks, and any form of violence. We, mike and pen pushers, thrive on the scent of blood and high drama. I didn't take up a 9 to 5 job in the hope that there would be many days like 13 December in my life: moments that make journalism truly one of the most engrossing and invigorating human experiences.

I have been distinctly fortunate to have had my share of such moments. The Mumbai riots and blasts of 1993, LK Advani's rath yatra, the Mandal agitation, the Shiv Sena digging up cricket pitches, Vajpayee losing a confidence motion by a single vote, tracking Kargil from inside Pakistan, suicide attacks in Jammu, earthquakes in Latur and Ahmedabad, interviewing Lalu in a cowshed, covering the Gujarat riots from the heart of the battle zone, the Akshardham attack, violence in the Uttar Pradesh Assembly, the Lahore bus ride, the nuclear tests, plane crashes in New York, tracking Mandela on the campaign trail, live election coverage with Prannoy Roy when Indian elections were five-day test matches, entering Taliban camps in NWFP, Sonia Gandhi rejecting the prime ministership, even watching Tendulkar's first first-class hundred: journalism has given me a ringside view to some of the most defining moments of the last twenty years.

And yet, nothing could have quite prepared me for 18 December 2005. The day before, 17 December, was a Saturday: the bloody Mary at the India International Centre is a temptation tough to resist, almost a Saturday ritual.

The attack on Indian Parliament in 2001: A genuine breaking news

Six months earlier, I had left the comfort zone of New Delhi Television along with my colleague Sameer Manchanda to set off on an adventure – an attempt to set up an English language news channel with the help of Television 18. It seemed pretty hare-brained at the time: one of the advertising agencies that made a campaign pitch to us said as much. 'Are you sure there is space for another channel? Who will really want to watch another channel, and how will you be different?'

Frankly, his cynicism was matched by my own sense of nagging self-doubt. Setting up a news channel, I was rapidly realising, was far more difficult than 'engineering' a 'big fight' in a television studio. Television is the ultimate team game: the challenge of setting up a twenty-four-hour news channel is to put together several diverse elements into a composite whole. A television anchor-reporter could afford to be the supreme individualist, basking in the fame and glory of being in the public gaze at all times. A hands-on television editor does not have the same luxury: the challenge is to examine the nitty-gritties that make all the difference: from the size of the ticker on the screen, and the spelling of a news flash to the constant flow of stories and dealing with the dreams and ambitions of young minds.

It wasn't easy, especially because the gestation period between planning and execution can often be frustratingly long. Worse, having been on air almost constantly for over a decade, the six months that it took to set up CNN-IBN were a bit like an extended *vanvaas* from the small screen. As a team, we'd done things remarkably swiftly, a tribute to the professionalism that is the hallmark of Television 18 and to the commitment of my senior colleagues: the studios were in place, we'd tied up with one of the biggest names in the news universe, the hiring had been completed, a rigorous training programme had been undertaken, the marketing campaign had been worked out and all systems were ready to go. And yet, we didn't have a launch date as we awaited final government permissions.

Which is perhaps why the Bloody Mary that Saturday afternoon in December 2005 was much needed. Alcohol has an ability to soothe the nerves, to allow the more worrying thoughts to drift away, to create a sense of well being and contentment. We had been going through 'dry runs' for several weeks now, fine-tuning our skills as a team. We'd been at it for a few weeks, maybe we could wait a while longer. New Year's day was just a fortnight away, and maybe a holiday in Goa would dispel the frustration of not being seen by the wider world.

Less than twenty-four hours later, we were, incredibly, on the air. At 6 am on 18 December, CNN-IBN was born: a channel, that perhaps a shade pompously, promised to be the 'temple of journalism', but also a channel whose tagline, 'whatever it takes', exemplified a hungry, passionate spirit of news-gathering. Journalism, as mentioned earlier, is often about good old-fashioned luck: just being at the right place at the right time can make all the difference. We were astonishingly lucky on day one, even if that element of luck had the familiar journalistic touch of blood and gore attached to it.

At around the time the channel was being launched, there was a horrific stampede in Chennai, a stampede in which dozens of people lost their lives. It was a tragic story, but also just the kind of story with dramatic visuals that was 'made for television'. We had a strong reporting team on the ground in Chennai and the visuals were first on the channel. We had hit the ground running, at a frenetic pace. As the breaking news tickers flashed, as the studio directors and producers ensured a seamless flow of images, as the news desk and assignment teams sustained the information barrage, as the graphics showed up on screen at the right moment, as the technical team were taking all the right steps, the months of unease and concern seemed to melt away: we could buy ourselves a drink because 'CNN-IBN *paas ho gaya*!' was the verdict.

The last time I'd felt like this was after my final law exams: a load had been lifted off my shoulders. Of course, we had a long way to go. A news channel isn't like a Bollywood film where sometimes first day, first show is all that matters. But at least we hadn't gone to black in the middle of a major newsbreak, our systems had been tested and, as a collective entity, we had

Dozens lost their lives in the Chennai stampede of 2005

proved that we were up for the challenge. Most importantly, we were on air and the world was seeing us, courtesy a fantastic effort by our distribution team in stitching up the cable operators. In the end, the beaming faces in the newsroom made it all seem worth it: we were like a bunch of college kids on the first day on the campus: excited, animated and lifted by a sense of having taken an important step up.

In the weeks and months ahead, there were many more equally exhilarating days, shaped by the efforts of an outstanding group of professionals that I have had the privilege to work with. As the day when barely four weeks after our launch, the television rating points showed us as the country's number one English news channel. While television ratings can be notoriously unpredictable, it was the quality of the journalistic content on Republic Day, in particular, which was far more satisfying. Our Republic Day programming which began with the president of India being interviewed by children on the lawns of Rashtrapati Bhavan ended with a first of its kind 'state of the nation' poll in front of the magical Humayun's Tomb. It was a memorable day, made even more special when the prime minister quoted extensively from our poll findings.

It didn't just end there. During the May 2006 state elections, our team of psephologists led by the redoubtable Yogendra Yadav got the Tamil Nadu election verdict almost spot on. TN elections have been notoriously hard to predict, and it can be even harder to deal with the aftermath. After all, if we'd got it wrong, there was a fair chance that we'd be blanked off the Chennai map. Now, our ever-energetic sales and marketing team was out and about to tell the world that we'd been the one channel that had its ear to the ground.

Prof Yadav, rather modestly, will probably attribute his success rate in election forecasting to luck. But sometimes, you get 'lucky', at other times you make your own luck. Sumon Chakrabarti, breaking the news on Bofors, accused Ottavio Quattorochi's accounts being quietly defrozen by the Indian government was one such story: it was possibly the biggest television story of that year, making it to the covers of leading national newsmagazines and being followed up by every newspaper. As Parliament was repeatedly adjourned, we could rejoice in a CNN-IBN 'impact' story. The union law minister didn't resign after the Bofors story. But at least two ministers in Uttar Pradesh had to resign after another major CNN-IBN newsbreak: Netas for Sale. The sting operation done by an independent group, DIG, in collaboration with our Special Investigation Team (SIT) was courageous journalism at its best: we had exposed how a minister was ready to courier drugs in his car for a price. The award-winning investigation showed the power of television – we could actually influence public opinion and make the system more accountable.

In the weeks ahead, the SIT led by VK Sashikumar, a tough and uncompromising journalist, would have many more news breaks to its credit. Their enterprise led them to launch 'Operation Water Rat', a seminal investigation that showed how thirteen years after the Mumbai blasts, it was still ridiculously easy to smuggle RDX into Mumbai's shores. Once again, the impact was immediate: the coast guard ordered an inquiry and agreed to tighten procedures.

'Impact' and 'investigations' were just two of the 'I's' in our DNA. There was the spirit of innovation, which saw us mount a nationwide 'Harvest Hungama', a celebration of Makar Sankranti of a kind which had never been witnessed on English news television. There was also the buzz of interactivity which saw *IBNlive.com* emerge as the premier news portal. There was the concept of inclusiveness, which saw the emergence of 'citizen' journalism, a revolution in itself. Suddenly, journalism was not just a one-way street: the viewer could now actively participate in the news process by sending pictures and stories.

Perhaps, the defining moment came on 11 July 2006, another of those crazy days in the news whirl when the lines between life and death, journalism and humanism begin to blur. As reports came in of a series of blasts on Mumbai suburban train network, we were all over the story like an army of ants. We were lucky again: one of our reporters, Jency Jacob, was on one of the trains where a bomb exploded. His first-hand account brought an authenticity to the coverage, the rest of the Mumbai team rose to the occasion with a series of stirring news reports. Citizen journalists came forward with their own stories. Quite remarkably that day, CNN International chose to stay with our 'live' coverage. It hadn't happened before: 7/11 was our version of 9/11 being played out to a global audience with a staunchly Indian perspective. If we were born on 18 December, we had truly 'arrived' on that bloody July day in Mumbai. As if to prove that there was life beyond journalism, we started a fund for the victims, a fund that helped several families get back on their feet.

A few days after the blasts, I was taking a flight out of Mumbai. Suddenly, one of the co-passengers came towards me and shook my hand warmly: 'Just wanted to say that you guys made a difference to the coverage of the Mumbai blasts. Thank you!' That's the kind of compliment a journalist lives for: not awards or material recognition, but the belief that in a small way, one can make a difference to the outside world. Today, as we add more channels to our news stable, the goal remains the same – to make a difference to the way journalism is practised, to make a difference to the lives of people. We haven't always succeeded, but at least we've tried our best. More importantly, we've enjoyed the ride.

RAVISH **KUMAR**

Ravish Kumar, 42, is Features Editor, NDTV India.

**THE AWARD WINNER**
REGIONAL AWARD, HINDI, BROADCAST

## A HOME OF THEIR OWN

WHILE SOCIETY DEBATES THE MERITS AND DEMERITS OF RESERVATION, RAVISH KUMAR EXPLORES THE QUESTION OF THE TRANFORMATIVE IMPACT OF THIS POLICY BY VISITING A HOUSING SOCIETY OF DALITS IN THE HEART OF DELHI.

## PERSONAL ACCOUNT

THIS WAS A STORY WAITING TO BE TOLD – NOT AT THE FAR END of some remote village but in the heart of the country's capital city, Delhi. My abiding interest in Dalit issues and my constant endeavours in trying to explore and understand some of these led me to this 'apartment complex' which has been made exclusively by Dalits.

I had sensed that here I might find answers to questions that had been on my mind for quite some time. Questions about the transformative impact of the policy of reservations. While the media and the rest of society have been engaged in a volatile debate on the merits and demerits of it, I wanted to explore the question from a different perspective. What happened to those who were beneficiaries of the policy – the first generation of such Dalit officers and other government employees? Did it change their lives substantially? What happened to them after they left service? Where did they live after their retirement? Did they manage to live harmoniously in the same cities in which they had previously lived in government flats, along with people of other castes? Did the new urban centres of modern India actually manage to break down the spatial politics of the traditional Indian village? Did people of all castes, creeds and religions, then, really come to live under the same roof when the trend towards building of housing societies began in Delhi?

This last one, of course, isn't a particularly difficult question. The answer to it is 'no, not quite', because barring some exceptions, on a large scale housing societies came up along the lines of caste, region, religion, profession and so on. The Mathur Societies, the Uttaranchal Societies, the Faizal Enclaves all stand as testimony to this fact. So given this harsh reality, my question still remained – where did officers and employees from the various government departments of Delhi go after they retired. Did they then have to go back to the so called '*malin bastis*' of their old villages? If not, then where did they go? While discussing such issues with a well-known Dalit writer and intellectual, whom I have known for a while, I seemed to find some answers to my questions.

He told me the story of Gaurav Apartments, a housing society that I had been frequenting for nearly five years now. I had been going there to visit a senior colleague of my wife, Nayana Dasgupta. He had never said that the apartment in which he lives is desperately waiting to narrate the success story of the Dalits. He never said to us that he was a Dalit, nor had we any reason to be inquisitive about his caste.

Anyhow, I had now found out the place where Dalit officers and other employees retired from the various government departments in Delhi had made a home for themselves. The story of Gaurav Apartments is therefore the story of their struggle to build the house of their dreams.

The outline of my special report was ready. Approval to go ahead with it from my editor was almost instant. And I was at the gate of Gaurav Apartment with my cameraman Shajilal, the next day. But things were not to be so simple. People in the apartment stood in our way with numerous doubts and questions. Mostly about our credentials. They wanted to know whether, as was the current trend in Hindi television journalism, we were going to make a sensationalised report, something like, 'look even the Dalits have made their own house and they do not need reservation!' They worried whether I was singling out their apartment for my report. They were concerned I would end up segregating them even further.

Their doubts, their suspicions and their questions were all valid. I had nothing besides the kind of reporting I have been doing on Dalit issues to establish my credentials regarding this. Thus, initially with several conditions attached, it was agreed upon that I would shoot only to the extent determined by them. Gradually, however, these conditions ceased to exist and trust began to build up between us. Soon, all the Dalit flat owners of the place opened their doors to our camera and their hearts to us. One began to introduce us to his daughter, another spoke of a son who was training to be a pilot. Someone told us about his childhood – how he was not allowed to ride a bicycle by the sons of Rajput zamindars; here his daughters-in-law are driving cars. Some told us about their children who went to prestigious public schools of Delhi, but who refused to identify themselves as Dalits any longer. So their surnames had been removed and in their places came the more ubiquitous surnames such as Singh and Prasad.

All the possible characters in a story of the aspirations of a rising Dalit middle class seemed to be present here. The story of the Dalit apartment complex was beginning to proceed from here. Dalit Apartments is the name I have given it but its current name is Gaurav Apartments. When this housing society was registered in the late 80s, its name was SC/ST Housing Society. However, the attitude of the people in the other housing societies that were coming up in Patparganj of east Delhi around that time, saw its name changed from SC/ST Housing Society to Gaurav Apartments. The story of my special report thus began to unfold.

One of the founding members of the housing society recollected his experience: 'There was a scheduled caste colony (Devnagar) in Karol Bagh. Some of us lived there but not everyone wanted to live in places like Devnagar. We wanted a better deal. We could have gone to the villages around Delhi. But

Gaurav Apartments: A home of our own

caste biases prevented us from going there. We thought – why not build our own apartments?'

Another member of the housing society told us, 'The building was registered in the name of SC/ST Housing Society. Hence, people from other castes did not want to join the scheme. We would literally go from door to door looking for a person belonging to the SC/ST community, trying to enrol them as members. We needed more and more people to ensure the inflow of adequate funds because many primary Dalit members were forced to leave due to lack of funds. We managed to enlist some members of the upper castes as well. But the likes of a certain Mr Srivastava left our society as he could not sustain the idea of living with Dalits.'

Nevertheless, the building was coming up. It had to. As the project proceeded towards realisation people from the upper castes gradually started coming in again. Out of 192 flats in this apartment complex, 25 were occupied by non-Dalits. However, property dealers continued to quote prices almost two to three lakh rupees less than market value. Then began a determined effort to keep the premises clean and shining to create a new image. An effort was also made to preserve its Dalit identity – a statue of Ambedkar was installed and a Buddhist vihara was constructed.

Residents of the society pointed to a very interesting aspect of this experiment. Even though caste discrimination had been faced while trying to build the apartments, within the apartment building, casteism was not allowed to flourish. For the upper-caste residents – an opportunity to live in a Dalit settlement for the first time.

People living within the society slowly began to forget the past. Caste-based identities began to dissolve into a new metropolitan identity.

It was to tell the world this unique story that this episode of Special Report came into existence. So that we may revaluate for ourselves the complex questions about reservations. This special report does not claim to provide ready answers to these questions. While on the one hand reservation did empower the Dalits to have a house of their own in the city and not have to go back to their old segregated *bastis*, on the other hand the struggle for an equal space and status still continues.

REJI **JOSEPH**

Reji Joseph, 42, is Bureau Chief, *Deepika Daily*, Kottayam.

**THE AWARD WINNER**
REGIONAL AWARD, INDIAN LANGUAGE, PRINT

## SHARING A POND WITH CATTLE FOR DRINKING WATER

THE CHAGLIYAR COMMUNITY OF GOVINDAPURAM VILLAGE IN THE DISTRICT OF PALAKKAD, KERALA, IS BEING INHUMANLY EXPLOITED BY ITS GOUNDER LANDLORDS. OSTRACISED BY SOCIETY, THE CHAGLIYARS ARE DENIED ALMOST ALL PUBLIC UTILITY SERVICES AND MANY BASIC NEEDS INCLUDING DRINKING WATER AND MEDICAL CARE.

## SHARING A POND WITH CATTLE FOR DRINKING WATER

FOR THE ATROCIOUS CRIME OF DRINKING WATER FROM HIS landlord's well, Perumal, a Chagliyar, lost his legs. On hearing that an untouchable had polluted his well, his landlord, a member of the Gounder community, flew into a rage and punishment was instantaneous. He cut off Perumal's legs and his goons threw the dismembered legs into the Meenkara river.

It was extreme thirst that made Perumal draw water from his landlord's well. Chagliyars are still treated as an untouchable caste and hard-dying social prejudices have always kept them at the bottom rung. As he was an untouchable, Perumal should have drawn his water from the waterhole where the cattle came to drink. He was a slave and a slave did not deserve to drink from that well. From the point of view of the landlord, an untouchable defiling his well was an unpardonable crime.

Chagliyars enjoy no better civil rights than yoked oxen. They are not to hold their heads high; they are not allowed to draw water from the wells belonging to the upper castes. A Chagliyar's tongue may get parched at the root; while working in the scorching sun, he might collapse in the paddy field and die. But fate has decreed that he should not slake his thirst if it means drawing water from the landlord's well.

Perumal was nineteen when his landlord cut off his legs and threw him into the streets, where he was to eke out a precarious living. He earned his keep by working as a cobbler. For years he could be seen moving on his haunches along the streets of the Kollamkode town. He may still be alive somewhere – a silent martyr who has to pay his daily respects to footwear to earn a living.

Savaraj and Muthukesh of Govindapuram colony are the descendants of Perumal and like Perumal they too reel under the yoke of caste-based discrimination. Resentment is smouldering in them. This is how they reacted to questions on their condition: 'Things have not changed since Perumal's days. Let alone drinking water, even for our clothing we are at the mercy of other people.' Incredible as it sounds, untouchability still persists in various forms even now in Kerala.

Members of the Chagliyar caste, now living in Govindapuram, M Puthur and Meenkara, have been little better than slaves all these years. In the little villages that lie close to Pollachi in Tamil Nadu there live hundreds of Chagliyars who are victims of casteism and social ostracism. They are excluded from social contact with others and are discriminated against in various ways.

At teashops, the Gounders are honoured guests and they are served tea in gleaming steel tumblers whereas, Chagliyars are not even welcome inside the teashop. A Chagliyar must crouch in the courtyard and drink his tea from glass tumblers. He should disappear the moment he finishes his drink. What if a Chagliyar wants to have his hair cut? They are unwelcome in barber shops, for contact with a Chagliyar's body will pollute the comb and the scissors. Tailors keep the Chagliyars outside their shops and stitch their clothes to approximate sizes. Chagliyars buy used clothes at wayside markets in Pollachi. At ration shops they do not get the full quantity of the rice and kerosene they are entitled to.

Chagliyars are not free to raise their voice against the injustices they are subjected to. A word of protest and a Chagliyar will lose his job. Loss of job means loss of the means of subsistence. The only way out in such a situation is to leave the place.

Chagliyars came to Palakkad from Tamil Nadu as bonded labourers in the 50s having been brought there by the upper-caste landlords. They work in the plantations of the Gounders, Nadars, Chettiars and Naikans – all high-caste Hindus. They toil it out in the fields of these wealthy classes.

The new generation may claim that untouchability is no longer practised in the country but the landlords' premises are out of bounds for the poor Chagliyars. They might draw water from the Palmyra troughs that store water for the animals. They must work from seven in the morning till late in the night for a pittance. A small quantity of rice water served in an earthen pot with the brim missing – a Gounder's generosity does not extend beyond that.

Ayyappan, a thirteen-year-old boy, sipped a cup of tea sitting with his legs crossed at the teashop near the Govindapuram bus stand. A Gounder beat him up for this 'temerity'. Murukesan, too, was beaten up. His offence? He collected watering from the landlord's tap instead of getting it from the waterhole for the cattle. Besides being beaten up, Murukesan was threatened that he would be done away with if ever the Gounders happened to see him again.

Even the Gounders' cattle enjoy precedence over the Chagliyars. A bull may come charging at him but a Chagliyar is not supposed to beat it off. All he can do is dodge the animal. The work he has to carry out includes watering the coconut palms, ploughing up the ground, and collecting cow-dung.

While at work the Chagliyars are supervised by the landlord's goons with the assistance of dogs. Bonded labour begins working at the age of ten and ends only with the slave's death. If a Chagliyar worker dies, the Gounder landlord will not even have the courtesy to pay a visit to his family. A dead

Chagliyar is not entitled to even a proper grave. Rains wash away the dead bodies from their shallow graves, which are scarcely more than one-foot-deep in the ground. Occasionally, the river carries a dead body to the Meenkara reservoir. Here, there is the danger of real pollution since the water supply schemes of Meenkara, Muthalamala and Kollenkode draw water from this reservoir.

Dark and blackened figures, the Chagliyars can only curse their fate. They do not have enough of any of the basic necessities of life – either cloth or rice. The Gounders' dogs and poultry are better fed than the poor Chagliyar children.

There are more than one thousand Chagliyars living in the Ambedkar Colony at Govindapuram. If they are to depend on the government water supply, they will have to do without water for twenty-eight days a month. So naturally they have to depend on the water tank for the animals in the Gounders' premises. The water supply scheme in Ambedkar Colony tells many a story of corruption. The pump there is not powerful enough to lift water to the hill-top tank. And there is nobody to bring the erring officials to book.

The black soil of Govindapuram is soaked with the Chagliyars' blood and sweat. The landlords raise corn, groundnut, pulses and paddy in the rich fields there. The coconut palms provide surprisingly high yield. But a Gounder would not let a Chagliyar benefit from even a windfall. He once thrashed Meenachi after tying her to a tree for taking a coconut. Her child once broke a ear of corn from the field. As the child was too small to be punished, the Gounder contented himself by awarding the punishment to Meenachi.

Having been treated like street dogs, the Chagliyars are migrating to other places for their survival. For example, Poomathi, wife of Kathirval of M. Puthur has left for Bangalore to work as a domestic servant. She simply could not put up with the segregation on the basis of caste. Poomathi once went to the Badrakali temple at Meenkara to fulfil a certain vow. She had brought with her offerings to the goddess – a bronze lamp worth Rs 750 and Rs 50 in cash. The priest stopped her at the threshold. He asked her to leave the offerings at the doorstep and leave the place lest she should pollute the whole temple. Poomathi burst into tears and cried out to the gods. With tears in her eyes she asked the priest: 'How come that neither my offering nor money pollutes you here but my presence does?' She never went to that temple again.

DURING MY YEARS AS A JOURNALIST SINCE 1996, I HAVE secured twenty-nine awards, including two international awards. I also received six national awards including the Ramnath Goenka Award last year.

The world as a whole is seeking hot news from the metropolitan cities. Those who do rural reporting have to admit that the media ignores or skips many important news developments from rural India.

Since the leading publishing companies in India are owned by businessmen and prominent industrialists, they regard newspapers as their product for the market and the media too concentrates more upon securing their popularity, while publishing news. In this context, a question asked by Dr APJ Abdul Kalam is relevant. At the Ramnath Goenka Awards ceremony, he asked whether there are any sincere journalistic efforts concerning the poor people in the country who are being ignored and suppressed in society. This vital question still lingers in my mind.

I received the Excellence in Journalism Award for my report about the Chagliyar community who face colour discrimination and racial separation.

Chagliyars are really slaves in the paddy fields and estates owned by big landlords. Entry of outsiders into the hamlets of Chagliyars is prohibited. It was really a great risk to enter into the huts and bring to light the problems of the Chagliyars, avoiding the notice of the armed goondas and Gounders. It was by living three days in strict secrecy along with my cameraman that the cruel aspects of exploitation of the aboriginals by big landlords and rich men was exposed. The report done by me during three days was one of the most remarkable experiences in my thirteen years of journalism.

Chagliyars are not permitted to talk with high-caste communities. In hotels, they have to eat their food only in plates set apart entirely for them. There is neither drinking water nor food made available to them. They are destined to be the slaves of the big landlords till the end of their lives. The natural question that came to my mind was, why has this tyranny not been eradicated?

With drinking water and food in my shoulder bag, I had to travel 40 kilometres in the 38 degrees heat to reach Pollachi on the borders of Tamil Nadu. Pollachi was selected as a resting place at night for the reason that there were no lodges to stay at Kollamkode Chagliyar village.

On the third day of our investigation, a Gounder received information that some media persons were camping in the Chagliyar colonies. The Gounder, who was also a panchayat member, came to the scene to question me. He asked me about our being there without permission. How could I have dared to enter a Chagliyar village? Smelling danger, I had to lie that we were a research team who had come there to study the lifestyle and ways of the Chagliyars. The Gounder was not convinced with my reply. The next question he asked me was equally hostile. He enquired why I had brought the photographer with me. I replied that to publish the research thesis as a text, relevant photographs were necessary as supporting evidence.

Looking at the facial expressions of the Gounders, I felt it was not safe to remain there for long. So, promising to return the next week to continue the research, we left the village. It was only when we reached Palakkad, 60 kilometres away, that I had a feeling of relief.

Journalism in villages is totally different from that in the city. Preparing investigative reports even now by living in the forest areas and rural villages is very difficult in the absence of phones and other communication facilities. But such a life is necessary to trace the pitiable conditions prevailing in the rural areas of the country.

It was in 1999 that I had reported on the sad plight of the cotton farmers in the Guntur district of Andhra Pradesh, who had been forced to to sell their kidneys to redeem their debts. They were poor people, who because of failed crops were unable to repay their debts. The moneylenders charged a very high rate of interest for the borrowed money. In such a situation the poor farmers sold one of their kidneys to repay the debts. Hundreds of poor farmers continue to commit suicide by consuming pesticides, in the grip of unbearable and huge debts.

The series of reports about the aboriginals residing in the forest areas where development schemes had never been implemented, included reports on problems faced by unwed aboriginal mothers in the Attapadi Hills of Palakkad district. For weeks I travelled across the Periyar forest to study the aboriginals who pursued cultivation in the midst of wild animals in the forest, to earn a living.

The reward for all my efforts was social recognition and the positive opinion of the readers. That gives more satisfaction than any award.

As soon as my reports about the sad plight of the Chagliyars were published, ministers and the district collector visited Kollankode and urgently made arrangements for procurement of food rations, electricity and drinking water in the area. Employment schemes for unwed aboriginal mothers were also formulated. The accumulated debts were written off. The mental satisfaction achieved by these measures implemented through the efforts of a journalist is heartening.

A journalist cannot dream of resting. Journalists are the guardians of democracy. If newspapers become extinct, our already weak democracy will become weaker still. To keep our country alive, newspapers should gather more vigour and strength. But, it is a cause of great anxiety that rural news is usually published on the inside pages of newspapers in a single column without getting the attention it deserves.

RITU **SARIN**

Ritu Sarin, 48, is Editor, Investigations, *The Indian Express.*

**THE AWARD WINNER**
JOURNALIST OF THE YEAR, PRINT

# FORGING THE SYSTEM

AS AN INVESTIGATIVE JOURNALIST, RITU SARIN PURSUES STORIES THAT OFTEN UNRAVEL CORRUPTION AND OFFICIAL MALAISE. IN THESE TWO STORIES ON THE ILLEGAL SALE OF SATELLITE PHONES TO THE SECURITY FORCES ON THE BASIS OF FAKE PAPERS, AND THE APATHY OF THE GOVERNMENT TOWARDS MISSING CHILDREN BRINGS INTO HIGH RELIEF THE UNSETTLING TIMES WE LIVE IN.

## FORGING THE SYSTEM

WHILE THE GOVERNMENT STILL GRAPPLES WITH THE unprecedented cyber-espionage in the National Security Council (NSC) Secretariat and the Naval war-room leak, yet another breach has been detected that puts a question mark on the checks and balances in the purchase of sensitive equipment by security agencies.

An investigation by *The Sunday Express* has revealed that a little-known Bangalore firm is suspected to have forged documents, fudged signatures of top government officials, and then used these to sell Thuraya satellite phones 'worth lakhs' to the army, central intelligence and state police agencies.

The investigation has revealed that the agencies which purchased these satphones from the firm, U & I System Design, include the Intelligence Bureau (IB), Military Intelligence (MI) and the Andhra Pradesh police.

One immediate fallout of this fraud, according to a confidential Home Ministry note accessed by *The Sunday Express*, is that there is a 'vacuum' in the security set-up as Thuraya phones are no longer available to security agencies. This is being seen as a serious handicap in the fight against criminals and terrorists who use Thuraya phones because of their superior features and ability to escape monitoring.

It was wireless adviser in the Ministry of Telecommunications PK Garg who first reported the forgery to the Vigilance Wing when a state police agency and the Central Reserve Police Force (CRPF) approached him with these fraudulent letters, which included one that had forged his signature.

Incidentally, the head of the NSC Secretariat, SD Pradhan, had also informed IB that someone by the name of Pradeep Chowdhary was fraudulently posing as an NSC 'security consultant'. U & I System Design admits the same man is their New Delhi based representative.

*The Sunday Express* has obtained a copy of a letter addressed to Pradeep Chowdhary and purportedly signed by National Security Advisor MK Narayanan appointing him as a consultant to the NSC for a three-year term as member (security and communication). And giving him the authority to 'coordinate with various Indian Embassies abroad'.

Shown this letter, Narayanan told *The Sunday Express* that it was forged. 'This is not my signature. No consultants in the National Security Council have been given appointment letters by me,' he said.

Narayanan isn't the only one whose signature was forged.

The signature of secretary, Department of Telecommunications, Vinod Vaish, and that of wireless adviser Garg were appended on letters, which company officials circulated to equipment suppliers. These say that U & I System Design has been granted 'exclusive operation' of Thuraya Satellite System and the rights to stock these phones.

'A few months ago, a state police agency, shopping for satphones, approached us with similar correspondence and we told them that it was forged ... It is apparent that supplies of Thuraya sets were made to intelligence and police agencies on the basis of such suspect documents,' said Garg.

Vaish, now member of the Telecom Dispute and Settlement Appellate Tribunal, said: 'Some months ago, I was informed of the forgery and about my signature being used. My immediate reaction was that a full-fledged inquiry should be ordered.'

When asked if an inquiry was ordered and, if so, what was its status, officials said they had no current update.

Investigations in Bangalore have revealed that while no company by the name of U & I System Design is registered with the Ministry of Company Affairs, the firm's 'development centre' located in Vyalikaval has been shut for almost two months.

The company's managing director, GR Itigi could not be contacted despite several attempts over a fortnight.

However, other company officials, including Itigi's wife, Shubha Pradha, confirmed the supply of Thuraya handsets to central and state agencies and admitted they employed a consultant by the name of Pradeep Chowdhary in New Delhi.

'Yes, we are providing telecom solutions to the Indian Army, the BSF and other agencies. Other questions can only be answered by my husband since we are facing some financial problems,' she said.

His employers admit that he is involved but Chowdhary claims his role was limited to the 'testing' of the equipment.

'The company has done nothing wrong and I am not aware of any allegations of forgery,' he said. Asked about his links with the NSC he added, 'I have done some work for them at some point but don't remember if I used their visiting cards or appointment letter.'

The fraud has had a disturbing fallout. A confidential Home Ministry note refers to the Bangalore-based company but makes no mention of the forgery.

While it says that police and security officials need to have Thuraya phones in operations against criminals and militants, it notes how a 'Bangalore-based company (an apparent reference to U & I) sold the sets to the army, the IB and the Andhra Pradesh Police but went out of business' even as Thuraya sets were being tested for the Central Reserve Police Force (CRPF) and the Chhattisgarh Police.

The Home Ministry note says that because of the 'vacuum' created by the previous vendor's exit, 'new players want to enter this field'.

'In the absence of any authorised vendor,' the note goes on to say, 'these sets are not available to security forces while they are being openly sold in the grey market in contravention of the Wireless Telegraph Act. It is learnt that some government organisations have also bought these from unauthorised vendors out of ignorance.'

Among the central police organisations, the CRPF, for one, has approached the government to allow them to legally import Thuraya sets. Says CRPF DG JK Sinha, 'We learnt about the forgery when we took the authorisation letters given by U & I to the DoT and were told they were not genuine. Our request to the government to allow fresh imports is under examination.'

PUSHPA DEVI LIVES IN LAXMI NAGAR, NOT MORE THAN A 30-minute drive from Nithari.* Like millions across the country, she, too, would have watched the details unfold – of missing children, their suspected remains, bone fragments and the rage of their helpless parents. For her, however, the story had an all-too familiar ring.

Not only because her daughter Poonam Lal went missing for ten years – she has since been traced – but it was her case that, five years ago, prompted the Supreme Court to issue a detailed list of dos and don'ts on missing children. It's a twelve-point list that, for all practical purposes, gathers dust as police forces, across states, plead helplessness when asked the question: where have the children gone?

In fact, missing children are the veritable black hole in law-enforcement. As an investigative series from several states will show, just like Nithari, the police failed to even acknowledge the problem, elsewhere, too, the typical police response being – the missing child is the parents' problem, not ours.

And if Nithari shows that a missing child may end up buried in a neighbour's backyard, the investigation shows that they can, as easily, end up in several places: as cheap labour in roadside shops, prostitutes in a brothel, exploited in the child-porn industry, kidnapped by the beggar mafia or even trafficked abroad.

Says Justice AS Anand, former chief of the National Human Rights Commission who, in 2005, sponsored the most definitive study yet of trafficking in women and children in India: 'Where are all these missing children? They have obviously not vanished into thin air. Children are our assets and we only do lip service to the problem of missing children. Even when a report of a missing child is lodged with the police, it is treated as a minor issue. Everyone thinks the child will show up and if that does not happen, the case is forgotten and closed.'

The reason is simple, say police officers: given that a missing child, by definition, is one who could move or be moved from neighbourhood to neighbourhood, city to city, state to state, any effort to track her involves coordination at all levels – in other words, between police stations and, in turn, between states. Such a mechanism just doesn't exist. This was exactly what the Supreme Court had called for.

---

* Nithari, a village in the suburban NOIDA, made international news headlines in December 2006 when the skeletons of a number of missing women and children were unearthed. A local businessman Moninder Singh Pandher and his servant Surender Koli were arrested on suspicion of murder.

Nothing captures the apathy to the problem better than the fact that nobody in the government even knows how large the issue is.

Yes, there are figures with the police – some states don't even have that – but these, officials themselves admit, barely tell the story.
Consider the following:

- The National Crime Record Bureau (NCRB), the nation's central crime research organisation, tabulates only cases of kidnapped children which it puts at 3,196 for the year 2005. Its website posts a list and pictures of 198 cases of missing persons, of which the number of children below 18 is only 66. Given that Nithari alone yielded a figure of at least 30 missing children, this shows how way off the NCRB data is.
- So it's not a surprise that even Minister of Child and Women Welfare Renuka Chowdhary rubbishes these figures. 'My feedback is that the figure of missing children runs into tens of thousands each year. I have asked all state governments to supply figures.' What she doesn't say is that she gave them two weeks but not one state has replied. What she underlines, however, is the alarm: 'I am apprehensive that another Nithari will happen if something is not done urgently.'
- Director of the Central Bureau of Investigation Vijay Shankar says that Nithari, for all its shocking revelations, isn't much of a surprise. 'It's only a symptom,' says Shankar, who is supervising a team of sixty officers probing the case. 'Nithari shows the larger malaise and a failure of the system to respond. There has been a serious failure on every count. Nithari happened because the police failed at the first point of delivery of justice, the administration failed with a just response thereafter and because society as a whole proved to be insensitive.'

Perhaps, the most reliable estimate of the problem can be gleaned from a 700-page report on trafficking of women and children in India prepared in 2005 by PM Nair, a former CBI officer, who is now with the United Nations Development Fund for Women (UNIFEM), sponsored by the NHRC.

As the key investigator for the project, Nair says he did precisely what Chowdhary is trying to do now. All state governments and Union Territories, except Bihar, Jharkhand, Punjab and Sikkim, supplied figures of missing children between 1996 and 2001.

The figures show a gradual upswing in the number of missing children in several states, led by Maharashtra (yearly average: 13,881), followed by Delhi (6,227) and Madhya Pradesh (4,915).

The average number of children declared 'missing' annually in the country was calculated at 44,476 – 122 each day – which included an annual average of 15,407 missing children from the six metropolitan cities. Of this, an average of 11,008 children remained missing. 'Where these children are is a serious question to consider,' the study said and pointed out that among metropolitan cities, only Chennai had a good track record for tracing its missing children.

'Many of these untraced children end up either being trafficked or in prostitution which is a huge law enforcement and social problem. Unfortunately, there is no synergy between what the government agencies and NGOs do to tackle the problem,' says Nair. His report draws disturbing linkages between missing children and trafficking and lists several case studies to illustrate this.

'Even if they (the parents) report to the police,' the report says, 'the police station treats it as a case of a child going missing. By and large, the police view in such cases is that it is the child who has run away or managed to disappear and they tend to pass the blame on to the child. Since (the evidence) showed that a large number of children who are reported missing are trafficked and thereafter, are being subjected to different types of exploitation, there is an urgent need to combat the problem.'

That's what the Supreme Court had done in the Poonam Lal case when her father and Pushpa Devi's husband Hari Lal knocked on its doors in 1988 for help in tracing his seventeen-year-old daughter.

Since the police failed to trace Poonam and the central government did not come up with firm proposals, a set of guidelines were eventually framed by the judges themselves. These include: mandatory publishing of the picture of the missing child in newspapers, on television, in public places like railway stations and inter-state bus stops; making inquiries from a long list of people and announcing rewards for tracing the child.

But more importantly, the Supreme Court issued directives to all state chief secretaries and police chiefs to set up a multi-task force to trace missing children in all states.

It's been five years since that order and the minister is now waiting for the states to respond.

IT IS NOT WITHOUT REASON THAT NEW DELHI IS CONSIDERED one of the most exciting world capitals to be reporting from and so exhilarating a posting that many foreign correspondents end up writing books on their experiences in India.

For even if you choose to ignore the strenuous screech of 'breaking news' on twenty-four-hour television news channels, look at what the Indian capital offers a newshound: enviable access to Cabinet ministers, many of whom respond to calls on mobile phones; frenetic political activity and a brazen show of skullduggery; economic expansion and business developments that the world media is now carefully mapping and a wide spectrum of human interest stories (fast becoming an endangered species) to pick from.

But the imponderables and dangers of functioning out of a pulsating dateline are as real as the flow of adrenalin which the constant news-flow in New Delhi generates.

The real challenge for a newshound – in a harsh and competitive environment where a *sarkari* denial is up for more animated discussion in the outhouse called the National Press Club than a news-break – is to sift a genuine 'lead' from what editors at *The Indian Express* describe as a 'lemon' and a potential scoop from a plant.

No less a challenge is to ferret out a high-value document from unsolicited 'secret' files that may arrive at the reception desk but which may be ingenious forgeries, or a manipulative source's test of your anxiety to rush to print.

For there are several instances when stories rejected for being unreliable or tendentious, appear with a bold display in a rival newspaper. Denials and legal complications follow.

After being in the business for long, one question younger reporters frequently ask me is: 'How do you land so many stories?' The fact is that a good story can parachute down, well, from anywhere. Besides the conventional sources – politicians, bureaucrats, lawyers, union leaders, activists – from mysterious 'deep-throats' and even prison birds.

Just the other day, I picked up the lead for an investigative series on government contracts being cornered by arms dealer Suresh Nanda's company from a copious letter written by inmates of Tihar Jail booked under the Official Secrets Act!

While cultivating conventional sources requires simple tracking and an element of tenacity, a more calibrated approach is required when an unidentified caller on the phone is revealing nuggets that ring true and he desperately needs to be kept talking. Reason: the source may never risk calling again.

My favourite 'deep-throat' story is the one on illegal foreign mail interception done by the Intelligence Bureau (IB). Someone, evidently, a senior serving official, tipped me off on how entire mailbags were daily loaded into the wide boot of an Ambassador (he gave the car number) and then ferried to the IB's counter-intelligence unit located near Khan Market.

Next morning, photographer Praveen Jain and I waited outside the international post office at Safdarjung Airport. On cue, the Ambassador rolled out of the post office with tags of some mail bags sticking out of the the boot! It drove directly into the IB's office. As we discovered while researching the story, this had been going on for years.

These days, sources find more ingenious ways of passing on information, probably realising that mobile phones are susceptible to interception. On occasions, sources have created e-mail addresses especially for the tip-offs and within hours, disenabled the same. Some useful leads came thus my way for scandals uncovered by *The Indian Express* on the purchase of surveillance and snooping equipment by the government.

The fact is that hundreds of crores are spent every year from secret service or unaudited government funds for purchase of equipment by intelligence and investigative agencies. But there is little or no media scrutiny of the issue as there is on defence purchases – albeit not nearly enough. The level of the Indian media's 'penetration' into the functioning of intelligence agencies remains abysmally low. In his recent book on the Research and Analysis Wing, Major General (retired) VK Singh detailed some suspect purchases and promptly got booked under the Official Secrets Act (OSA).

Stories written by me which received commendation for the Ramnath Goenka award, include those on surveillance scandals, national security breaches and functioning of investigating agencies.

The first was a series on the inroads made by a private firm, Shoghi Communications, in the supply of snooping equipment to the intelligence and military establishment. The company was discovered to have forged documents during supply of encryption equipment to the National Security Guards (NSG) for which the Central Bureau of Investigation (CBI) issued an advisory to all government agencies. It was only when *The Indian Express* reported the case that the National Security Council (NSC) responded and the Military Intelligence issued its own order blacklisting the firm.

However, even eighteen months after the CBI's action, the same company was picked by the Defence Research and Development Organization (DRDO) for the supply of frequency demodulators and surveillance monitors for the prestigious Rs 570-crore 'Divya Drishti' project, conceived as an electronic system for tracking hostile airborne targets after the Kargil operation.

The scandalous aspect of the deal was that the three companies short-listed for tendering were all part of the Shoghi network, with the same family ownership and address. The decision of the Ministry of Defence to blacklist the firm resulted in its equipment lying unclaimed at the Customs warehouse and 'Divya Drishti' being delayed inordinately.

The blacklisting of the company by the MoD made me curious to find out how many other dubious entities face a similar ban. Since we had a few pages of the blacklist, landing the entire database was not difficult. In all, following a first-ever nationwide compilation, the MoD ran up a list of 118 blacklisted vendors and arms suppliers, which curiously included an entire country, the former 'Yugoslavia'.

This is how serious the malady is, with no one knowing whether the MoD has ever revisited or updated its blacklist.

There are several such instances where government agencies sniffing a scandal chose to look the other way. Shortly after the exposes on cyber-espionage in the NSC and the Naval war-room leak, *The Indian Express* unplugged a scam about a little-known Bangalore company, U & I Systems, using the forged signatures of top government officials, including the National Security Advisor MK Narayanan, to commence supply of Thuraya satellite phones to the Indian Army, the Intelligence Bureau and state police agencies.

When *The Indian Express* visited the story, we discovered that the wireless advisor was already aware that his signatures (for exclusive supply of satellite phones) had been forged, but merely informed the vigilance wing of the Department of Telecommunications (DoT).

In the meantime, a part-time employee of the company continued posing as a 'consultant' to the NSC and was brandishing an 'appointment letter' bearing the signature of the NSA, another clever forgery. Following *The Indian Express* intervention, the Delhi Police lodged a criminal case against the company, and the Home Ministry and DoT followed suit by ordering formal inquiries.

New Delhi is the headquarters to all investigative and intelligence agencies. So there is a constant flow of information about cases these organisations want publicised. Over the years, the number of so-called specialised agencies – such as the Serious Fraud Office, the Financial

Intelligence Unit, and the National Technical Research Organisation – have mushroomed but this has not been matched by a conscious effort by the media to cover them as regular beats or trace their evolution in an age when cyber crime and terror funding have become serious concerns internationally.

The good news is that, finally, there appears to be an effort to share intelligence within the labyrinthine network of agencies, though rarely does one acknowledge the good work of another. They prefer to pass off leads or hard intelligence as the handiwork of their own sleuths.

A case in point is the Volcker investigation handled by the Enforcement Directorate (ED). *The Indian Express*, inadvertently, played a role in the turn of events. The newspaper was the first to expose arms dealer Vipin Khanna's son, Aditya, as the chief facilitator of money transfers in the surcharge scandal, reaching Indian beneficiaries.

Once Aditya was confronted with the evidence collected by the ED from Iraq – obviously on misplaced legal advice – he managed to board a London flight despite prior instructions being issued to immigration authorities to suspend his passport.

The story on Aditya Khanna's 'escape' evidently raised the hackles in the finance ministry. The errant immigration officer was suspended and urgent instructions were issued to ensure Vipin Khanna did not similarly leave the country. The day the instructions were issued, the older Khanna was detained at the international airport while boarding another London-bound flight. Aditya would return to New Delhi to assist the investigations but two years on, despite frantic petitions before the Supreme Court, the Khannas, have not managed to get their impounded passports back.

The spin-off probe from ED's impressive Volcker investigations proved to be equally, if not more, significant. While scrutinising the money trail of companies used to route the oil-for-food pay-offs, the ED traced a web of off-shore companies linked to the Khannas and informed the MoD about the suspicion of huge money transfers being linked to defence deals (including the Denel deal) and sales of arms to Pakistan. The MoD immediately issued an advisory barring them any access to the defence establishment.

It is believed that in the clutches of the ED, members of the Khanna clan revealed how the major players in the arms business had, for decades, been using a similar modus operandi. It may be a coincidence, but events moved fast thereafter. The CBI raided all the big fish – among others, the Khannas, the Choudharys and the Nandas – and the Income Tax (IT) authorities conducted massive search operations on the Nanda establishment.

The onslaught of multiple agencies on a clutch of defence dealers was to break their stranglehold on the shadowy business of arms trading. But as events subsequently unfolded, the CBI's actions proved to be selective.

In fact, a careful tracking of the politics of the CBI requires scrutiny not only of what it holds up for prosecution but more importantly, what it puts on the backburner (one glaring example is the case of Mayawati's disproportionate assets, the investigation of which was tied up four years ago). Covering the CBI also requires a careful tracking of cases which the government, through the Department of Personnel and Training and the law ministry, does not allow the CBI to appeal against (the Bofors case which was stymied at every stage by politics, the last being the shocking episode of the Law Ministry advising the CBI not to appeal against the denial of extradition to Ottavio Quattrocchi from Argentina).

To return to the arms dealers: while the CBI registered cases against some major players, it has done nothing to bring back Sudhir Chowdhury, one of the biggest boys in the business, who was conveniently out of the country when the CBI raided his house. Despite claims to the contrary, CBI bosses have not made even a perfunctory attempt to reach him in London. Even after he was named as one of the middlemen in the Barak missile case, Interpol has not been alerted about his whereabouts.

This pick-and-choose attitude of the CBI has been exposed often by *The Indian Express*. Even while lodging cases under provisions of the archaic Official Secrets Act, the agency has been quick to respond to dictates of 'higher-ups' as it did in the VK Singh case but failed to take cognisance of very damaging leaks in the MV Rao case, which *The Indian Express* chronicled. This story is revealing for the manner in which a senior technocrat (he was a director with Bharat Heavy Electricals Limited) was involved in a conflict-of-interest situation that would benefit an arms dealer, Suresh Nanda.

On that occasion, the Prime Minister's Office (PMO) alerted agencies about how Rao was posing as an adviser to the prime minister himself. When the Delhi Police raided the 'imposter's' residence, they recovered a huge pile of secret documents, including minutes of meetings of the Cabinet Committee on Security (CCS) and internal correspondence of the MoD and the defence minister on purchases.

Despite Nanda and Rao being on CBI's radar, agency officials say they are holding back an (Official Secrets ACB) action since the Delhi Police has, in over a year, not handed them authenticated copies of the documents.

Confronted with such glaring instances of wrongdoing, followed by inaction, bureaucrats and police officials find convenient shields to hide behind. The CBI's favourite excuse, especially with an increasing number of cases having transnational implications, is the Letter Rogatory (a request to another country for assistance in a criminal case) and scores remain unanswered, thus holding up probes. Officialdom has also perfected the art of passing the buck, by placing the onus of a controversial decision or oversight on another department or ministry.

There is now a powerful tool in the hands of the media to pierce such stone-walling tactics or the recalcitrance of babudom. But unfortunately in the three years of its existence, while everyone from activists, lawyers, businessmen, harassed consumers, property-owners, even students have effectively begun to use the Right to Information (RTI), journalists are using it with superficial success. On the other hand, its counterpart legislation in the US (The Freedom Of Information Act) has been invoked by media organisations to bring out secrets of state into the public domain. In India, no media organisation has yet invested in an RTI cell.

To place the effectiveness of the transparency regime ushered in by the RTI in perspective: for one, it is a system that works. Some departments (like the PMO, CBI) promptly respond to requests while others (Delhi Police, law ministry) obfuscate attempts to obtain sensitive information. The attempt should be to apply for information duly covered under the provisions of the Act; to make the queries specific instead of roving inquiries, and doggedly follow up rejected applications with appeals.

The use of any information act invariably proves to be a test of the resilience of the appellant versus the obstructionist attitude of the government department holding the information in its custody. Thus, an interesting game of roulette is played out with RTI requests.

Information we sought on political asylum cases resulted in the request being bounced from the Ministry of External Affairs to the Home Ministry, over a dozen times. Similarly, a request to the Department of Expenditure on quantum of secret service funds was injudiciously routed to every government department, resulting in an impressive pile of 'nil' responses from ministries like Child and Women's Welfare and Urban Development, which have nothing whatsoever to do with secret service funds.

The trick for scribes is to use the RTI Act not as an end-all solution but as a vehicle for better-informed journalism. While some RTI replies may result in a complete story, the data and material provided by the government should ideally, be backed by independent fieldwork and reporting. There is no substitute for that.

That's the challenge, and the excitement that keeps a reporter like me always interested in the chase.

ROHIT **KHANNA**

Rohit Khanna, 39, is Executive Producer, Special Investigations Team, CNN-IBN.

**THE AWARD WINNER**
POLITICAL REPORTING, BROADCAST

## NETAS FOR SALE

WITH POLITICIANS STOOPING TO LEVELS BEYOND AN ORDINARY CITIZEN'S UNDERSTANDING, ROHIT KHANNA WITH A DEDICATED INVESTIGATION GROUP EXPOSES IN A STING OPERATION HOW POLITICIANS WILL DO ALMOST ANYTHING TO MAKE EASY MONEY.

IN UTTAR PRADESH, THE LINE BETWEEN 'KHALNAYAK' AND 'Vidhayak' has been blurred for a long time. The more you break the law in Uttar Pradesh, the greater the likelihood that you will go on to become a 'lawmaker'! Murder, rape, kidnap, extortion, assault, arson, theft, fraud – Uttar Pradesh politicians have been accused of them. But when confronted, pat comes the line, '*Yeh to hamare khilaaf virodhi party ki saazish hai!*' (This is a conspiracy hatched by a rival party.)

Jamshed Khan, Mayabhushan Nagvekar and Amitabh Thakur, in 2005, were part of the Dedicated Investigation Group (DIG), and they wanted to expose the farce. If people with criminal backgrounds were getting into politics, there was only one way to prove it.

Get it ON CAMERA!

This is how they did it ...

In 2005, Mehboob Ali, Samajwadi Party MLA from Amroha was minister of state, Backward Classes Welfare in Mulayam Singh Yadav's Uttar Pradesh government. The DIG first got to know Sabir Ali, a confidant of Mehboob Ali. Sabir's job description suited DIG well – he brought 'favour-seekers' to the minister.

This is how the encounter went:

**DIG:** You are totally 'open' with mantriji?

**Sabir:** Yes, he has men who collect 'donations' within the constituency. But don't worry. Even though the work you want done is for elsewhere, there's nothing to be hesitant about.
(Sabir was soon 'singing' about Mehboob Ali's other businesses, making some serious admissions.)

**DIG:** Tell us a bit about the minister's petrol business.

**Sabir:** The usual – mixing solvents in petrol. Preparing spurious petrol.

**DIG:** Is he still doing it?

**Sabir:** Openly! Who can stop him now? It's his main source of income.

**DIG:** How many petrol pumps does he own?

**Sabir:** Two.

Working closely with the DIG, was VK Shashikumar, head of CNN-IBN's Special Investigation Team (SIT) and further fact-finding followed. This led to Ajabpur *thana* in Moradabad district, which like police stations across India, keeps records of people with criminal backgrounds in its jurisdiction.

Serial Number 26, History Sheet No. 8A documents Mehboob Ali's crime record. His brother, Mehmood Ali, alias Bhura, also has an active criminal history sheet – No. 18A.

The DIG and SIT also found out that during an earlier tenure as Uttar Pradesh's Wakf Board minister, Mehboob Ali awarded himself a ninety-nine-year contract for a piece of Wakf Board land, on which he built a hotel. That hotel is now another steady source of income.

The DIG then received another shocking admission from Sabir Ali: Mehboob Ali was involved in drug trafficking as well.

**Sabir:** Yes, we deal in opium. That's a fact. In heroin as well. Mantriji is on the look out for 'parties' to sell to. He has to make money as well, isn't it?

It was crucial for DIG and SIT to explore Mehboob Ali's track record. Clearly, involved as he was in petrol adulteration, land-grabbing, drug-trafficking and being a 'history-sheeter' with the police, Mehboob Ali was a perfect candidate for a Special Investigation.

After 'gifting' Sabir Ali a cellphone and Rs 5,000 in cash, on camera, we finally met the man himself.

Number 10, Kalidas Marg in Lucknow was Mehboob Ali's official residence, a massive bungalow with sprawling lawns. Mulayam Singh, then Uttar Pradesh chief minister, and other ministers, were Mehboob Ali's neighbours in the high-security area.

It could have been a scene from *Omkara:* the minister, dressed in kurta-pyjama with a heavy moustache, slumped low in his cane chair, chain-smoked and enjoyed blowing smoke rings endlessly. He sported several mobile phones, surrounded by police guards armed with machine guns and rifles – henchmen and hangers-on – in kurta-pyjamas or safari suits, hovered around.

Caught with cash on camera

Jamshed Khan and Mayabhushan Nagvekar decided to use the 'onion peeler' approach, stripping the minister bare, layer by layer. They first established that he did entertain petty favour-seekers, as long as they were prepared to pay to get the 'job' done.

**M Ali:** What do you want?

DIG: We have an acre of land in NOIDA, in Sector 126. It's being acquired. We have to stop that from happening.

M Ali: I can get it done.

(A few queries later, Mehboob Ali got quite direct; his choice of words, not too pretty.)

DIG: Sir, could you get some transfers done as well?

M Ali: I can handle transfers, postings as long as I know you well. If I know you well, if it's something underhand, if you need someone to be beaten up, if someone needs to be mother-f ... ked, it will be done!

DIG: Could you organise government jobs?

M Ali: Whatever you say!

At the next meeting the DIG reporters asked Mehboob Ali to help get a lawyer appointed as a district government counsel, and for the transfer of a police sub-inspector. The minister agreed but also took an 'advance'.

DIG: Sir, we've brought some money as you had asked. It's not much ...

M Ali: How much have you brought?

DIG: Rs 20, 000, sir.

M Ali: I'll take it ... no problem.

Maybe he was superstitious, but the minister didn't actually touch the 'dirty money'. It was another henchman, Ishtiaq, who emerged from behind a curtain to accept the money from the DIG reporters in full view of the minister. Mehboob Ali also clarified that when the 'job' was done, five lakh would be the full 'price' of the district government counsel's appointment and one lakh to get the police sub-inspector transferred.

We almost forgot he was an elected representative of the Samajwadi Party in the Uttar Pradesh Assembly, a minister in the Mulayam Singh cabinet. He had taken a bribe and asked for lakhs more to fix land deals, transfers and postings. So, the rumours were true. It was time to push the envelope further.

DIG: Sir, my friend is from Goa. He has something to discuss with you.

M Ali: Tell me.

DIG: Sir, we host 'acid' parties for tourists in Goa during the holiday season.

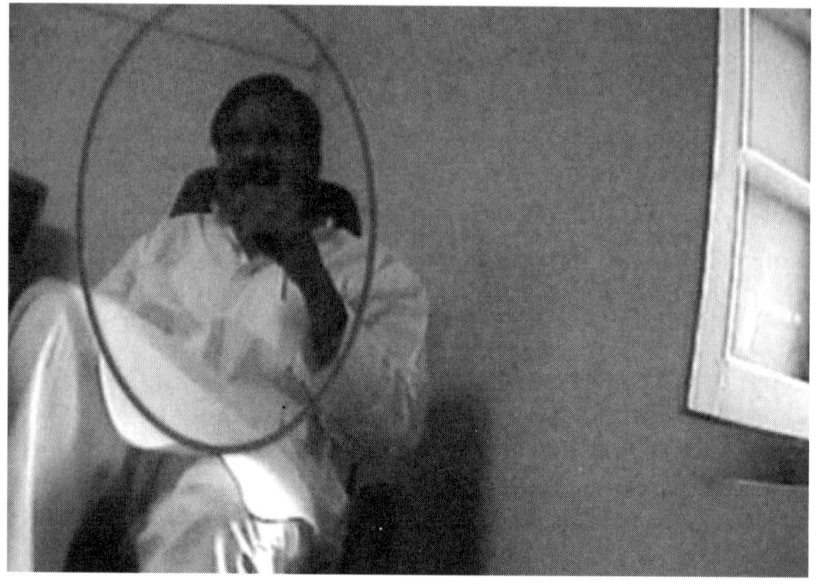

'Get the money and I will get it done'

**M Ali:** What is there in 'acid'?

**DIG:** Acid contains heroin and LSD.

He appeared cautious, but was not offended by a direct proposal from someone who had for the first time revealed they were 'drug traffickers'. He listened as they spelt it out.

**DIG:** Our drugs travel from Barabanki to Lucknow. Then to Delhi and then Goa. From Delhi we have secure routes. But in Uttar Pradesh there is police pressure – we need your help.

**M Ali:** What help?

**DIG:** We need someone to take the drugs from Lucknow to Delhi.

**M Ali:** *Arre*, this is your business, leave me out.

(He then dropped a bombshell.)

**M Ali:** Why don't you contact Beni Prasad's son? His son is supposed to be in the drug trade. Rakesh Varma, our prisons minister. He is from Barabanki, so it could be true.

(Mehboob Ali clearly indicated to us that former Union telecommunications minister Beni Prasad Verma's son Rakesh Verma was a drug trafficker. Rakesh Verma was then minister of prisons in the Uttar Pradesh government and

Mehboob Ali's colleague. Barabanki district, just 30 kilometres from Lucknow, is a known hub for growing and processing opium.)

The minister gradually seemed to be getting interested in the matter.

**M Ali:** Yes. I could do this. Nobody will question me. I could deliver the stuff.

**DIG:** It's worth five crore, sir. We need to take it from Barabanki to Delhi.

**M Ali:** What will you be sending?

**DIG:** Heroin till Delhi. From there it goes to Goa for the foreign tourists. You can have your share.

**M Ali:** How much?

**DIG:** You tell us.

**M Ali:** I just have to take it up to Delhi?

**DIG:** Yes sir, in your car. No one will question a car with a '*laal batti*'!

(Mehboob Ali then made a stunning admission, totally exposing his links with the narcotic trade.)

**M Ali:** I'll give you the name of a person from Barabanki. You could buy from him.

**DIG:** A person known to you?

M Ali: Yes, yes. But first ...

**DIG:** First?

**M Ali:** Get the money and I'll get it done.

(The minister, at his official residence, clearly said, 'show me the money and I will get your work done'. Not only would he facilitate the pick up of heroin from a friendly supplier in Barabanki, he would also allow the use of his official car to transport the drug consignment to Delhi.)

He also spelt out his price.

**M Ali:** For every one crore, I'll take twenty lakh.

Meaning ... for every heroin consignment worth one crore, Mehboob Ali would take a cut of twenty lakh!

DIG and CNN-IBN's Special Investigation Team decided at this point that the nexus between crime and politics in Uttar Pradesh had been comprehensively exposed. There was no attempt to meet the minister again.

The stories were first played on 15 February 2006. Three days later,

Mehboob Ali resigned from Mulayam Singh's Uttar Pradesh Cabinet. Bharat Petroleum instituted checks at their pumps after hearing that Mehboob Ali, who ran two BPCL pumps, was involved in petrol adulteration. The Uttar Pradesh Assembly set up an inquiry committee to examine the matter.

It was also important for this investigation to demonstrate a zero bias. To show there were no vested interests backing the reporters, it was important to expose politicians from across the political spectrum.

So, Jamshed Khan and Mayabhushan Nagvenkar also approached Anil Kumar Maurya. Maurya was then the Bahujan Samajwadi Party MLA from Rajgarh, 40 kilometres from Varanasi. A first-time MLA, Maurya was essentially a businessman. He owned the prominent Hotel Surabhi on the outskirts of Varanasi. He also produced Bhojpuri films, which, with their raunchy content run to packed houses in Uttar Pradesh and Bihar giving a guaranteed return on investment.

The DIG went to Maurya representing a fictitious NGO that was planning to work in his constituency with a fictitious budget of Rs 2.5 crore. On camera, Maurya agreed to take 5 per cent of that amount as 'protection' money. On camera, he took an 'advance' of Rs 10,000 for the deal.

But what was more shocking in the case of Maurya were the other details that emerged on hidden camera.

First, he revealed that he was involved in hawala rackets. He described in detail how he was an expert at transferring black money, admitting he had strong links with 'hawala' racketeers in every major centre of the country. He claimed to have transferred hundreds of crores over the years, without ever being detected.

He also revealed that election tickets could be 'bought'. Talking about the BSP, he explained that there were 'rates' for the various constituencies. An aspiring MLA would have to pay Rs 50 lakh to Mayawati's party if he wanted a ticket from a BSP stronghold. It would cost five lakh if a candidate wanted to contest from an opposition stronghold – just for the 'prestige' of getting an 'election ticket'!

Maurya also admitted to regularly hunting sambhar, cheetal – animals on the protected list. He and his brother even brought out and showed off the guns they used.

The investigation also brought into its net, Sumaru Ram Saroj, then BJP MLA from the reserved constituency of Kerakat near Jaunpur. Again, the DIG went to Sumaru Ram as a fictitious NGO planning 'construction work' in his constituency. Sumaru Ram was soon ready for his 'cut'. In return he would ensure that the 'NGO' could function smoothly in Kerakat. On camera, Sumaru Ram took an 'advance' of Rs 5,000 from the DIG.

Investigations conducted by CNN-IBN, especially in the area of Barabanki, uncovered the criminal histories of others from the political class in Uttar Pradesh. Most prominent was the twenty-year criminal 'history sheet' of former Uttar Pradesh minister Sangram Singh Verma. Page after page of massive A2 size police documents, revealed that he was deeply involved in drug-trafficking. Details maintained with complete diligence. Yet the police seemed never to have enough to actually put the 'history-sheeter' behind bars.

We are into 2008, as this is being written. Mayawati now rules Uttar Pradesh. Mulayam is plotting his return. Rahul Gandhi is touring the state, promising to bring in change. With no one prepared to take him seriously, what about the protagonists of our story? Here is the post-script to the story, which seemed to have conclusively exposed the darker shades of politicians like Mehboob Ali and Anil Kumar Maurya.

In the 2007 Uttar Pradesh Assembly elections, both Mehboob Ali and Maurya were thought worthy of election tickets by their respective parties. Mulayam Singh chose to disregard evidence that clearly suggested Mehboob Ali's involvement in drug trafficking, and Mayawati chose to back a self-confessed 'hawala' operator! And not to be out-done, the people of Uttar Pradesh, using their one unassailable weapon, the vote, in what was arguably a free and fair election, voted both Mehboob Ali and Anil Kumar Maurya back to the Uttar Pradesh Assembly!

As the producer of the investigation, I was a spectator to the courageous work of Jamshed Khan and Mayabhushan Nagvenkar. They, along with Amitabh Thakur of the DIG, spent months travelling through Uttar Pradesh's grey criminal zones looking for and confirming 'leads'. Law-enforcement officials, preferring to stay anonymous, also proved helpful.

Then began the risky task of approaching each MLA maintaining the thin veil of a fake 'identity', banking on the sheer overconfidence of the MLAs that they would never do a thorough check on the DIG reporters sitting before them, with hidden cameras rolling. They also had to ensure that they had sufficient 'on-camera' evidence of corruption and admission of criminal activity.

They did all this with complete integrity and in good faith. It was truly the journalism of 'courage'.

CNN-IBN's Special Investigations Team added layers to the investigation returning to all these places with cameras, regularly, visiting local police stations, social activists, even former drug peddlers to give further credibility to the already damning material on hidden camera.

The recognition that came to the overall effort, a project that CNN-IBN called 'Netas For Sale', by way of the Ramnath Goenka Award for

Political Reporting was a huge shot in the arm for those who had been a part of it.

Crime in politics is clearly one of India's biggest illnesses. Those involved are no fools. And they are powerful, many having their private militias, many misusing the might of the state machinery, since in so many cases they are the State! Clearly, journalists will have to often use robust and innovative measures to expose such persons. They must be judicious and responsible, with all the checks in place. But surely, till things change, I for one, do believe and say – more power to Jamshed Khan and Mayabhushan Nagvenkar and the preferred tool of their trade – the hidden camera.

SADHANA **MOHAN**

Sadhana Mohan, 50, is Editor-in-Chief *AIDS Buzz*, an initiative by Partners in Development, New Delhi.

**THE AWARD WINNER**
REPORTING ON HIV-AIDS, PRINT

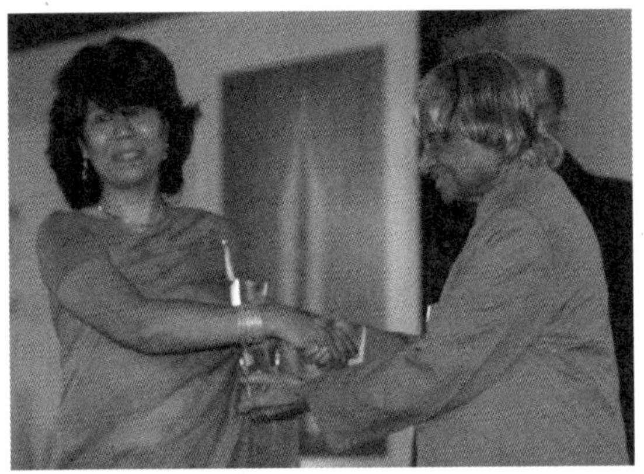

## PRAYERS, GOD & SEX

RELIGION AND RAUNCH MIX FREELY AT THE ANNUAL KALIYAR SAREEF MELA IN UTTARANCHAL. SADHANA MOHAN TRAVELS TO THIS FAMOUS SHRINE OF THE SUFI SAINT WHERE BEHIND THE GLITTER OF THE MELA RISKY GAMES ENDANGERING PRECIOUS LIVES ARE BEING PLAYED.

COME EVENING AND A BEVY OF BEAUTIFULLY 'MADE UP' WOMEN flaunts what it has among festive revellers at the little-known Kaliyar Sareef Mela in Kaliyar, a village 5 km from Roorkee in Uttaranchal.

The 'women' unleash their charms with wild abandon. A wink here, a pinch or a caress there, followed by an invite – '*Bas 100 rupaiye loongi*,' (I'll charge only Rs 100). Some minor haggling, and the deal is struck. The rendezvous point could be a tin-roofed shed or the mango-scented jungle.

Sex sold by eunuchs and men who have sex with men (MSM) appears to be a big-time activity outside the religious precincts of Saabir Paq, a Sufi saint, whose shrine attracts tens of thousands of people each April, the auspicious month of Rabi-ul-uvval as per the Muslim calendar.

The 12th day of the month is particularly auspicious. And so crowds reach a peak here from the 11th day of the month through the 16th day. They come from various parts of North India, and even from Pakistan. There is a strong belief that Saabir Paq grants their wishes. Legend says the saint went hungry for years on end even as he distributed food to all and sundry beneath a luscious gulnar tree, a short distance away from the shrine. He did so because God told him to distribute food to others, without asking him to partake of it.

Walking around the venue on the 18th day of the month, one saw young and old men, businessmen and farmers, cooking chicken curry and biryani in mega-sized pots over wood-fire. A delicious aroma assailed. '*Deg chadayaeinge*' (we will offer this food at the shrine), '*khud khayenge aur khilayenge*' (will eat and also share with others), Abdullah Bhai told us as he lovingly stirred tender chicken pieces and gravy. Between 30-40 family members and friends sat around him. They had come from Sigroda, a village about 30 km away in a privately hired bus.

Nearby, a young man proposing to distribute biryani had to lug up the pot containing over 20 kg of the stuff on a tree, and notch it up still higher when hungry hands became obstructive and greedy.

In an atmosphere of religious fervour, men, women and entire families rub shoulders with eunuchs and MSM, who too are out in large numbers. 'Nearly 50 per cent of visitors are eunuchs and MSM,' a housewife from Trilokpuri, Delhi, estimated.

Young Mukesh (name changed), of Muzaffarnagar, who sells cheap ornaments at the fair each year, has seen a spurt of sexual activity in the market. Gaudily dressed eunuchs sashay around, teasing and inviting men, and striking monetary deals.

Sunny, a fellow hawker, concurs. Hẹ too has been accosted, touched, and offered services in exchange of Rs 50 or Rs 30. 'More than 400 tents, maybe half of them occupied by eunuchs and MSM, crop up on the adjacent grounds. The eunuchs dance and do mujrah (a form of dance) well into the night. They too come to offer prayers and goodies to God, but the side business is quite intense. The spin-offs are good; you can see them squandering money. We've seen them give Rs 500 notes to beggars – they are good at heart,' say Mukesh and Sunny.

They live 8-10 people in a tent. And for sex, the mango orchard opposite is a perfect getaway; so are the open fields next to the canal running through Kaliyar.

Who's the Man!

As we drove back from Kaliyar, our car driver asked the peer educator accompanying us: 'What would we have done if one of the Punjabi eunuchs in the shrine had become abusive?'

The peer educator, an MSM working as a peer educator with eunuchs, laughed: 'You tell me, you are the mard (male).' The driver looked sheepish.

Our peer educator had scored a point. He was definitely a 'greater man' when it came to this issue.

'At the most, they would've threatened to go naked and I would've asked them to go ahead. You should also tell them that. Why is everyone so upset at this prospect?' laughed our escort.

On a rough estimate, reveal insiders, a person could have 10-12 clients a day. The stay at Kaliyar could last a week or 10 days; some go back home for a few days and come back to camp.

Mohammad Shafir, a stage dancer who attracts viewers to *maut ka kuan* (a death well), says *kapde wale* (people in clothes-a term used to denote cross dressers) often join him on stage and are followed by young men when they leave the stage. They charge about Rs 50 from a client.

Crowds thin out by the 16th day of the month and the eunuchs and MSM reportedly leave by then. We spot only a handful of eunuchs during our visit. We try speaking to Anjali, a eunuch, who keeps averting her face and refuses to talk, fearing we are some kind of 'authority'.

Inside the mazaar (shrine), Aslam, a 40-year-old eunuch, who's been at Kaliyar for the past 12 days, says he's been coming to the shrine since the age of 12, when his grandfather would bring him. 'Each year I have come here without fail,' he says, folding his hands and pointing towards the mazaar.

He comes here to say prayers, seek peace, and do some good work. Ten years ago, when Aslam did not expect to survive a fever, he set off for Kaliyar. Halfway through he felt better, and upon reaching Kaliyar the fever vanished completely. 'All that's wrong is sorted out when one visits here,' he says.

Aslam knows about AIDS and says sex is to be avoided. Leena, a Punjabi school-educated eunuch from a professional background, enjoying tea with a maulavi is outraged at the topic of sex work. 'We live in homes and do not philander. We are neither men nor women – you are referring to men, they indulge in sex,' she says.

Development, Advocacy and Research Trust (DART), a community-based organisation working with MSM in Delhi and adjoining areas, that made the rounds of the fair when festivities were at a peak, found that over 1,00,000 eunuchs and MSM visited the mela. DART was seeking to ascertain eunuchs and MSM's vulnerability to sexually transmitted infections. It claims to have contacted 1,823 eunuchs and MSM and have had 100 of them respond to written questionnaires.

In all, 72 of the 100 respondents admitted that they came to the mela for sex work. Also, 78 per cent said their last sex act was unsafe receptive anal sex. Receptive sex acts per person can theoretically far outnumber penetrative sex acts and are therefore an indicator of greater vulnerability to HIV.

Further evidence of condoms being out of favour came with 93 of the 100 respondents saying they did not use condoms in their last sex act and 48 per cent of them saying they did not use condoms because they did not enjoy sex when they had them on.

Behind the glitter of the mela at Kaliyar, risky games endangering people's lives are being played. Nowhere in the din is there a word about HIV/AIDS or condoms. An Amitabh Bachchan-Shah Rukh Khan hoarding in Urdu exhorts people to give polio drops. On the road to Kaliyar, huge advertisements on the walls invite men to improve their virility and seek treatment for sexually transmitted infections. That's all – not a line about safe sex or HIV.

Innumerable herb sellers do brisk business at the fair. They can perhaps be roped in as key persons talking to people about HIV and STIs. This could be a starting point for talking about protection and care.

'*MAIN KAPDE PEHENTA HUN*' (I WEAR CLOTHES), THE THIRTY-something 'man' sitting next to me in an Indica taxi replied, affably. Rakesh Sahai, our photographer on assignment, looked incredulous. 'Oh, yeah?' he chipped in from the front seat.

Having figured out the sense of what the 'man' was saying, I quickly and matter of factly brought Sahai on board, explaining that 'clothes' was a synonym for cross-dressing.

Had you seen me talking, you would have thought that for me, cross-dressing was, well, as mundane a phenomenon as seeing a woman drive a car.

Making our 'man' comfortable was critical to the success of our assignment, as this, you must have guessed, was no ordinary assignment. As every journalist worth her or his salt knows, 'sources' must be respected and put at ease. Extreme sensitivity to the source's feelings and situation is needed for the person to open up all before you, a veritable stranger. It is only when the source speaks from the heart that you get a clear grip on his or her story, a prerequisite for you, in turn, to write from the heart and communicate the story to my readers.

The 'man' I've been talking about, self-professedly, had sex with men and could be classified as one belonging to the community of men who have sex with men (MSM). He was working as a peer educator with *hijras* (eunuchs). The term 'peer' seemed to imply that he was a *hijra* and one gathered, during the course of some light, non-judgemental talk, that he did often stay and move around with *hijras,* offering *badhai* (blessings) on occasions, such as wedding and childbirth. And yet, he was married to a woman and had a daughter.

Let's call him Dalbir, for the sake of convenience. He was my first contact to my self-assigned job on hand – visiting and writing about a religious fair, *Kaliyar Sareef Mela,* thronged by MSM and *hijras*, a sizeable number of whom were said to be selling sex through the auspicious month of *Rabi-ul-Uvval* as per the Muslim calendar. The visit led me to write the article 'Prayers, God and Sex' in *AIDS Buzz*, a bi-monthly newsmagazine reporting events and trends regarding the AIDS epidemic in India. This was the lead article in the January 2006 edition of *AIDS Buzz.*

Understanding Dalbir's sexual identity had me in a tizzy but I tread softly around, learning about a husband who had sex with men and also lived as a *hijra*. He loved talking, had plenty of humour, and was forthcoming and direct in supplying information.

Grappling with Dalbir's reality was just a bit part in what you might call a day-long foray into an unreal world. For the world of *hijras* and MSM is exactly that for most of us in society and mainstream media – a little-known-about world.

It wasn't the kind of assignment that you go to with a song on your lips. I knew I wanted to research the event and write about it. It promised a peep into a 'different' reality and just like every filmmaker aspires to make a film that is 'different' from the rest, a reporter too likes to uncover the unseen and draw attention to areas requiring urgent attention.

But here I was going to interact with *hijras* and MSM on intimate issues of sexuality without having ever met *hijras* before and having had only a cursory kind of interaction with MSM. I knew I would delve a bit into the background of these people to give them flesh and blood in my writing, something I learnt to do for all interviewees early on as a cub reporter with *The Statesman.* Would they open up? It was critical to develop a certain amount of rapport with them before shooting off questions about sexuality. How was I going to do that with a population I knew little about and with whom I had no common ground?

*Hijras*, as one knew from childhood, come knocking on people's doors on festive occasions and behave aggressively and crudely, sometimes threatening to undress to extract a hefty *baksheesh* (donation). How was I going to talk to so many of them about sensitive issues like sex and HIV-AIDS, asking questions such as whether they came to the fair for sex, how many sexual partners they had in a day, did they use condoms, etc?

The prospect of a unique story excited me deeply and despite a niggling sense of trepidation, there was no looking back. In fact, in twenty-four years of practising journalism, seeing a story at the end of a tunnel has meant never going back despite all odds. This has involved travelling alone to remote areas such as Ziro in Arunachal Pradesh to examine the AIDS scenario there, travelling with *hijras* and a photographer in tow along the Mumbai-Thane highway at midnight, interviewing commercial sex workers on Delhi's GB Road, in Kolkata, and at highways between Bharatpur and Jaipur at night.

A pleasant April morning, thus, saw me up at 5 am and out of my Greater Kailash Part II house in a taxi. I picked up Rakesh Sahai from his house in Mayur Vihar. Dalbir was waiting for us at Shyam Lal College in east Delhi. We set off for *Kaliyar Sareef Mela* in Kaliyar, a village five kilometres from Roorkee in Uttaranchal, a journey of five hours from Delhi.

Turning left from Roorkee, we came upon Kaliyar. A long canal ran along the middle of the main road of the village. A little ahead, slightly short of the fair venue, we passed some brick homes and guest houses. A couple of cyclists and a few people were going down the road.

We saw a *hijra* walk by and called her. We invited her to sit with us at a small teashop and talk to us. Dalbir helped break the ice by making some preliminary introductions and asking the *hijra* where she was from. Suspecting us to be associated with the police or the local administration, the *hijra* refused to open up and kept turning her face away from the camera.

This was exactly the kind of response I had feared. But I knew that once I was on 'ground zero', I would leave no stone unturned to get all the information I wanted from as many people as need be. I would talk to shopkeepers, fair visitors, priests, and any other possible source of information to get a sense of what was happening at the fair.

Hesitantly, two hawkers at the fair acknowledged a spurt of sexual activity in recent years. One of them had been accosted, touched and offered sexual services by a cross-dressed *hijra* for a price between Rs 30 - 50. Gaudily dressed *hijras* and MSM sashayed around the fair, teasing and inviting men, and striking monetary deals, the hawkers told us. They described to us in detail the living arrangements of *hijras* and MSM, the getaways for sexual interludes, and the kind of money that *hijras* spent at the fair.

Families at the fair said that nearly 50 per cent of the visitors there were *hijras* and MSM. Apparently, tens of thousands of people visited the shrine of Saabir Paq, a Sufi saint, in April. The fair is organised outside the shrine.

Inside the shrine, we saw Leena, a Punjabi *hijra* looking like a beautiful woman in a blue *zari*-work sari and elaborate make up. She appeared stand-offish and it wasn't easy to approach her but with Dalbir at my side, I went up to her, asking initial gentle questions about her background. Her brother was a senior bureaucrat in Punjab and she had completed school education.

Leena was livid at the topic of sex work. 'You are talking of *khairgallas,* men who indulge in sex. We are *paanwalas,* we live in homes and do not philander. We are neither men nor women,' she told me sternly. She seemed to suggest she was castrated, but I dared not ask. Dalbir explained that *paanwalas* were *hijras* who lived by strict rules and some of them were castrated. *Khairgallas,* he explained, were non-castrated and into multi-partner sex. They also mischievously went to collect money during celebrations from homes allocated for this purpose amongst *paanwalas.*

Sahai was about to click an interesting picture of Leena and a *maulavi* (priest) sipping tea together when the *maulavi* objected. Sahai immediately complied. We could not risk inviting trouble. 'That would've been the best shot – a *maulavi* offering hospitality to a *hijra*' – Sahai told me later. But a seasoned news photographer knows his limits. Had he jumped the gun, the assignment might have ended there and then, with some commotion to boot. It goes to Sahai's credit that we got reels of good pictures with no feathers ruffled.

Spotting Aslam, a *hijra* from Delhi, inside the shrine, I decided I could have a one-on-one talk with him. He didn't look threatening and I was looking for time alone with an interviewee. I feel one gets the best out of a person when talking one-on-one. It is more comfortable for a person to be addressed by one person. He can respond better than he would if two or three people were talking to him and the flow of conversation remains in the reporter's hand without having any other person interject or throw a suggestive question. I couldn't have come this far without Dalbir but he was now superfluous.

Would I have been able to write such an article in the mainstream media? I don't think so. And that is something that I would like media houses to take notice of and rectify. After all, there is a wide world beyond Delhi and state capitals, and also beyond the not-so-real world of politics, bureaucracy and corporate public relations.

Let's see what might have happened if I had been a newspaper staffer. I might or might not have got the chief reporter's nod for the outstation trip. The reason for refusal? Not one, but several. Maybe, my 'beat' was active so I needed to be in town, maybe there was staff shortage so a reporter could not be spared, or maybe the 'news' element was not strong enough, after all, there were no hard facts about HIV-AIDS incidence (death, morbidity, etc.) that I was going to bring back with me. *Hijras*' and MSM's vulnerability to HIV-AIDS or the general population's vulnerability to HIV was going to be the key message of the story. 'Not newsy enough to merit the expense and the space' would seem the most likely verdict. Or somebody might have rubbished the attention being given to *hijras* and MSM by the AIDS programme and media reports.

As a freelancer, going to the fair by cab becomes a daunting proposition because you pay yourself. If you bus it, you and the photographer would need to spend the night there, in which case, again, you pay out of your pocket. The usability of the piece is not assured, more likely that considerations of the type mentioned above will prevail and the piece will be dumped without you hearing of it again. If at all it is used, you are paid a measly amount that doesn't compensate the effort, let alone the actual expenses.

The reason I am listing my angst is that good journalism, especially writing human interest and developmental stories, is not receiving the encouragement it deserves from established media houses. Pick up any newspaper, big or small, and you will see the datelines are either the national capital or state capitals. Other towns figure only when there is a tragedy!

I could write and publish my article because I was Editor-in-Chief of *AIDS Buzz*, a publication brought out by Resource Centre for Sexual Health and HIV-AIDS (RCSHA), which was a project of the UK government's Department for International Development (DfID). RCSHA was set up to provide technical assistance and help build the capacity of India's National AIDS Control Organisation (NACO) and its counterparts in the states called State AIDS Control Societies (SACS). *AIDS Buzz* was conceived as a method of facilitating an exchange of information on what was new and happening in the AIDS field across NACO, SACS, and NGOs.

We, at *AIDS Buzz*, thought we would examine on-the-ground initiatives in the AIDS field in various states or write about interesting trends so that people working in the area of AIDS were stimulated to think anew and take stock of developments in states other than the one they worked in or at the national and international level.

*AIDS Buzz* was the lone journalistic enterprise in an AIDS programme full of 'programme people'. RCSHA, therefore, deserves to be lauded for an extremely professional handling of the publication.

There was complete journalistic autonomy or editorial freedom. You smelt a story anywhere in the country and you could go there and do it or get somebody to cover it. No one messed around with your judgement of a story idea or the content of a story. You also got adequate time to research a story and related documents.

It goes without saying that journalism of the highest standard was being practised in terms of honesty and accuracy of facts, sensitive writing, and gathering of information from various sources to cross-check information and rule out exaggeration.

Usually, there is great mistrust between programme people (read NGOs working in AIDS or development) and the media. Here, however, we set a path-breaking example of synergy between programme managers and the media.

Programme people at RCSHA opened the doors wide to their discussions regarding work, reports, and analysis of what was happening on various fronts. I participated in these frequent discussions and picked up whatever ideas I thought were worthy of journalistic perusal.

Working in close tandem with programme people meant seeing their point of view, understanding all the efforts that were being put into the programme, and then raising pertinent issues in articles. Often, you had to read several heavy reports to get to the heart of a matter for you found a certain theory or view in circulation and not sufficient clarity on why it was in circulation or the specifics of the situation.

You didn't want to offend people working in the area of HIV unnecessarily though you did want to offer constructive criticism. Criticism simply for the sake of criticism is easy, something that a regular media person is programmed to do. But criticism or, rather, suggesting a direction that makes sense to people in the field and is received well by them (as against in-your-face, armchair stridency) requires a lot of hard work and analysis and sensitive writing, one learnt on this project.

Let me give an example of an article I wrote highlighting the incidence of sexually transmitted infections (STIs) in children as a result of child abuse. The article was written in the wake of the Nithari village episode in Uttar Pradesh's NOIDA, where twenty-two lives were lost before the country woke up to the issue of child abuse.

A colleague at RCSHA mentioned having seen slides of extremely small kids, aged two years or so, with painful STIs as a result of sexual abuse. That was all the information one had in hand.

From here, on to understanding STIs in kids, figuring out the approximate number of children affected by STIs in the entire country each year and why these figures were not heard about, advocating for early and correct treatment of STIs in kids so that they are spared unnecessary suffering, highlighting the fact that an early visit to a specialist could also lead to treatment that reduces the risk of HIV, and drawing attention to the important fact that the national AIDS programme, ignored the sexual route of HIV transmission in children and only addressed parent-to-child transmission – all of this was quite a task.

Writing the story in an extremely readable way was part of the challenge, not to mention the immense attention given to terminology acceptable to NGOs, for example, preference for the term STI to the term sexually transmitted disease (STD) to avoid the use of the word 'disease'.

STIs, sex, and HIV-AIDS because of links to sexual behaviour and use of protective devices such as condoms, etc., are kinds of 'hidden' issues, information about which is not public knowledge. Contrast writing on these issues to filing an exclusive crime story or an excellent column on crime and you find that though the latter might require considerable effort in terms of cultivating 'sources', they do not require extensive research into 'amorphous' areas.

A small idea can lead to a big story. RCSHA, though not a large media house, allowed every idea, small or big, to flourish and held high the flag of courageous journalism.

## SHEKHAR VASANT **DESHMUKH**

Shekhar Vasant Deshmukh, 36, is a freelance journalist. He is Fellow, Henry J. Kaiser Foundation's International Health Journalism Project, and is also consultant, Johns Hopkins University's Media Advocacy Programme.

**THE AWARD WINNER**
REPORTING ON HIV-AIDS, REGIONAL, PRINT

# CAN LIFE BEGIN AFTER HIV?

A POIGNANT YET POSITIVE STORY OF A YOUNG WOMAN, LIVING WITH HIV-AIDS FOR THE PAST MANY YEARS – AND HOW SHE FORMED THE FIRST 'POSITIVE WOMEN'S NETWORK'.

IN NAMAKKAL, A SMALL VILLAGE IN TAMIL NADU, A YOUNG Bride, P Kousalya, had barely settled into her marital home when her husband started showing symptoms of full-blown AIDS. She was tested immediately. But by then it was too late. She, too, had acquired the virus. Quite unlike many others in her situation, Kousalya did not weep or wallow in self-pity. She was determined to live. Gradually she moved from this quiet, sleepy village to the bustling metropolis of Chennai, about 150 kilometre away and formed the first 'Positive Women's Network'. This was in May 1994.

2 March 2006: 'Positive Women's Network' (PWN), Shanti Apartments, Avenue Road, Nangabakkam, Chennai is a place of hope in this middle-class locality. Group discussions, seminars and public-awareness programmes go on side by side in this office. You may find one member of this organisation counselling another. Some narrate their stories on the phone; others brief international visitors on the organisation's work. In short, all have a common goal – to live life positively. Kousalya is the president of this group. Kousalya is a typical south Indian girl with a dusky complexion and sharp features. She is in her late twenties and has been living with HIV-AIDS for the past thirteen years. But that has not daunted her. Her grit and determination shine through her eyes as she continues to provide hope and strength to countless positive women around the country.

She is an example of how one can turn obstacles into opportunities. Her upbringing had infused her with self-belief. She says: 'I lost my parents at an early age. My maternal grandparents took care of me. My grandpa looked after my upbringing and was very affectionate. My environment taught me self-belief and self-discipline. Knowingly or unknowingly good habits were nurtured during my childhood. I learnt to stand on my own without expecting anybody's support.'

She has no complaints about her life. She does get upset when she recalls the time she was diagnosed and was ostracised by her neighbours and others.

Doctors would not treat her opportunistic infections once they learnt she was HIV-positive. When her husband died, she was pregnant. Her child was her hope. But another tragedy awaited her. Her baby girl, too, died within a few months.

She had nothing more to lose. Gradually, she got in touch with several women who had been similarly infected in Namakkal. She met people from a self-help group. This group transformed Kousalya's life. For the first time, she was educated on HIV-AIDS – how it spreads, how it can be prevented and about anti-retroviral drugs. She too formed such a group. She gathered enough strength to be able to narrate her life's story to the media. After this interview, the Tamil Nadu Network of Positive People contacted her.

She decided to leave Namakkal and move to her uncle's place in Chennai.

There, she was introduced to TNP Plus and INP Plus, organisations formed by people living with HIV-AIDS. She set up the first 'Positive Women's Network' in October 1998 with twenty HIV-positive women and their children. She had to fight against all odds. She was refused a place for her organisation. Even when she managed to find a place, due to the social stigma attached with HIV-AIDS, she could not put up a board of the outfit she started.

Today, more than 5,000 women across the country are members of this organisation. In Tamil Nadu members work through a well-coordinated network to provide medicines, nutritious food and counselling. They take up issues and come to the rescue if they find rights of HIV-positive people being violated. About eight months ago, four patients died in the district hospital in Namakkal, allegedly due to negligence. Kousalya took up the issue. Initially, the authorities did not pay any attention but eventually they had to replace the doctor and restart the medical care unit.

Kousalya now travels extensively, educating people across the world about the issues of HIV-positive women. Earlier she could speak only in Tamil, but now she has learnt English as well. A beaming Kousalya and her members occupy centrestage in posters in several institutions and organisations working for HIV-positive people. 'I feel I have miles to go,' she says.

'The main challenge is to create a positive environment for positive people. What they require most is the support that will boost their confidence. But unfortunately this is what they lack. I am very lucky that I met good people and found a positive environment. Our aim is to create an environment of hope for these psychologically and physically shattered people.'

Kousalya likes to work at the AIDS ward at the Tambaram sanatorium near Chennai. Several projects are undertaken through PWN to impart education to these women about AIDS, give them support and provide nutritious food to them and their children. Kousalya visits them regularly.

When I ask her if she had ever thought that her life would take such a dramatic turn one day, she answers, 'I wanted to buy a bicycle in my childhood but could not get it because of poverty. Now, my efforts prompted my uncle to gift me a scooter. When I am in Chennai, I use this scooter to commute to my office. All this gives me immense joy and a much-needed will to live my life as I am.' Kousalya has left her past behind as she concentrates on the future.

FIVE YEARS AGO, A MEDIA WORKSHOP ON AIDS IN DELHI WAS my first chance to come face to face with organisations working with AIDS patients and HIV-positive people. One such organisation, Care and Support Centre for HIV-positive children, was the venue of our practical training. The centre, besides treating children between nine months and fifteen years, also provided for their lodging, food and education related needs. We tried to acquaint ourselves with the children. Naughty, playful and yet some of them looked mature beyond their age. We were told that most of these children belonged to the lower economic strata. Many had become orphans after their parents died of AIDS and, as it happens in such cases, relatives had refused to take responsibility for them. There were others who had been abandoned by their own parents or were admitted here because their parents couldn't afford expensive treatment.

Her sparkling eyes, fair and chubby face had made her a favourite with everyone. Though only nine months old, unlike most children of her age, she did not mind sitting quietly in a stranger's lap and that too, without throwing tantrums. I took Gudiya in my arms. Her eyes were playful and I took an instant liking to her.

Gudiya was born in a nearby slum. Her mother had died of AIDS three months earlier and her father was dead too. When relatives abandoned this nine-month-old baby, a social worker came to her rescue and admitted her to the centre. Was she HIV-positive? There was no way of finding that out till she turned one-and-a-half years old. No HIV test was possible till then and everyone at the centre was hoping and praying that Gudiya would test negative.

All alone, orphaned even before she knew the importance of a family, abandoned by her own near and dear ones – this little child was suffering, despite no fault of hers. What would happen when she grew up? What about her education, employment opportunities? I couldn't bear to think that she had a gloomy future ahead of her.

Holding Gudiya in my arms, I realised that AIDS was not a medical problem alone; it had created social, cultural and economic complications in society. Those suffering due to this disease were also living with guilt, with their acquaintances despising them. It had created a void within society; the decay was not merely physical but mental as well. Surely, this wasn't an issue that one could erase after a news article or a workshop? This issue required sensible and sensitive handling.

Gudiya made me delve into the issue of HIV-AIDS; she inspired me to report on this crisis that our society was facing.

Regularly published reports, interspersed with figures, have helped journalists keep themselves informed about AIDS. Interacting with these children, I realised that while discussion pertaining to facts and figures had been going on for several years, those infected with HIV-AIDS have always remained in the background, neglected and uncared for. The media, too, has stressed upon the figures and graphs and almost always chose to ignore the patient – their pain, distress, remorse, joys, problems and solutions; their longing for life has never been part of any fact-file, neither have these been topics for discussions.

For any kind of reporting, tackling the bureaucracy, politicians, police are challenges that most journalists face. While writing on AIDS, the biggest challenge for a journalist is mentally connecting with this sensitive issue. It is perhaps easier to beat the system than triumph over one's own mind. News has become too demanding these days, deterring journalists from delving into an issue for a longer period of time. In fact, no journalist can now afford to linger on a story. No matter how significant the issue is, the reporter is compelled to hop from one story to another in search of news that sells. Accustomed to such a scenario, it is indeed a daunting task to persuade oneself to connect with an issue as grave and as complex as AIDS.

The people one meets while reporting these stories are living in constant fear of death; their despair is far deeper than that of others. No sensitive individual can remain indifferent to the plight of these people. The Delhi workshop created a permanent impression regarding the dilemmas and difficulties of HIV-positive people in my mind. It was difficult to erase the pain.

To understand the issue, I toured the length and breadth of the country. During these trips I realised that reality had two faces – there were two sides to each story. The failure of the system, dejected individuals, failed NGOs – I saw all this and much more during my trips through Maharashtra, Uttar Pradesh, Andhra Pradesh, Tamil Nadu, West Bengal, Manipur and Rajasthan. The situation was perhaps worst in the villages of Uttar Pradesh. In several villages in the state, no one had ever heard of AIDS and in places where people had heard of the disease, no one wanted to cremate the body of a person who had died of it, fearing that the minute the body was burned, the AIDS virus would come out of the body and spread throughout the village. In Manipur, it was worse than an animal's life for the HIV-positive drug users who had decided to undergo treatment at the rehabilitation centres. In Andhra Pradesh's Guntur Medical Hospital, no doctor was prepared to treat an HIV-positive pregnant woman. Worse, post delivery the doctors refused to touch the child. Another infected person, a maid, was treated like an untouchable.

In Sangli-Solapur in Maharashtra, after the death of her husband due to AIDS, a woman was forced to lead the life of a destitute with even her son disowning her. What could have been an ideal vehicle for sex education, the sex museum, was all but defunct. The Hindu pilgrim centre of Varanasi was sitting on an AIDS time bomb – the culprit in this case was an increased tourism-related activity. Shockingly, both the government and NGOs chose to look the other way.

This dismal reality had its silver lining as well – tales of human dignity in the face of antagonism and rejection. These were tales of courage and grit where individuals living with HIV-AIDS reached out to people like them and created awareness regarding the disease and its socio-economic implications. Fighting against societal odds, an elderly father-in-law was supporting and taking care of his HIV-positive daughter-in-law. A professor and his student toured villages to spread AIDS awareness, sans any financial assistance from any national or international agency. For them, this was a part of their social commitment. Every week, along with his discourse on the Holy Quran, a maulavi also talked to the local youngsters about HIV and AIDS. A doctor treated HIV-positive persons free of cost. These were stories that rarely made headlines.

HIV and AIDS spelled death and certain organisations and individuals were propagating this for their vested interests. If this was one aspect of reality, there was a positive side to the same reality too. This was the aspect that I tried to bring to fore through my articles. As a journalist this was my chance to support people who represented the positive face of the issue. The entries I sent for Ramnath Goenka Excellence in Journalism Award represent both sides of the story.

Reporting on AIDS, I stumbled upon two stories that left a lasting impression on my mind. The first one took me to Mohanpur, a sleepy hamlet on the Gorakhpur-Kushinagar road. Here, I met a woman who was living with HIV-AIDS. Her husband had died of AIDS and her in-laws had severed all ties with her. Worse, her children had been taken away from her. 'Mother has a dangerous disease, she has sinned. You should not meet her,' this is what they had been told. It was the life of an untouchable for this woman, as the entire village had cast her off. With almost no physical strength, her first requirement was an anti-retroviral treatment. But lack of financial help had made it impossible for her to reach the nearest AIDS care centre at Lucknow. She had no will to live. Teary-eyed she asked: 'What was my fault? Did I deserve this life?' In the crowd that had gathered around, there was a fifteen-year-old boy. Spotting him, she started weeping helplessly; he was her son. I tried asking him a couple of questions, but he refused to answer – it was as though the woman sitting before him was a stranger. With her son refusing to even acknowledge her, she was crying inconsolably. It was a sight that remains etched in my mind forever.

The second experience concerns my Chennai trip. It was by chance that I had attended a musical programme organised by the Indian Network of People living with HIV and AIDS. The event, titled 'HIV & Me', was a platform for HIV-positive people, living in the four southern states of Andhra Pradesh, Tamil Nadu, Kerala and Karnataka, to interact with ordinary citizens and to declare their HIV status. It was their attempt to traverse fear and choose self-belief and thereby, take the first step towards undergoing treatment. This was also their bid to create awareness regarding AIDS as well as to dispel the myths and stigma associated with it.

As everyone settled down, the programme began. Soon, the tempo increased and the audience was all charged up to hear the evergreen numbers of matinee idol of yesteryears, MG Ramachandran. At one corner stood a group of HIV-positive people from Tamil Nadu, swaying to the popular melodies. Soon, they started dancing to pulsating beats and there came a time when some of them came to the gangway to dance to the film music being played on the stage. Shortly thereafter, the entire group was dancing. They did not have any inhibition. These were happy and carefree faces enjoying that moment to the hilt. It was an unusual scene. The people, whom most in the audience would have described as dejected, were dancing with joy – the ecstasy written on their faces belied their pain and struggle. They just wanted to live every moment. For me, this was a moment of realisation: The solution to their crisis was in their own hands. It was this sense of positive approach that I wanted to highlight in my articles on AIDS.

Had I not prepared myself to connect with the pain of AIDS and HIV, I would have surely missed an opportunity to meet individuals who live life against all odds; I would have never understood their approach, their behaviour. And thus, I would have missed the purpose of journalism.

SHIVANI **NAIK**

Shivani Naik, 28, is Principal Correspondent, *The Indian Express*.

**THE AWARD WINNER**
SPORTS JOURNALISM, PRINT

# WILLIE HETARAKA AND THE RUGBY FACTORY

INDIA'S FIRST FOREIGN RUGBY COACH, KIWI WILLIE HETARAKA IS DETERMINED TO TAKE THE COUNTRY'S TEAM OF FIFTEEN HIGHER AND HIGHER.

## WILLIE HETARAKA AND THE RUGBY FACTORY

WHAT DO YOU DO WHEN SOMEONE TELLS YOU, WITH AN ostensibly straight face and in one single breath, that he's lived in Bombay his whole life but has never heard of Mumbai? I, for one, blinked twice, and made the quickest of mental notes to get my handset checked for clarity.

But Willie Hetaraka comes from Bombay Hills, a township 40 kilometres southeast of Auckland, in New Zealand. India's first foreign rugby coach was soon admitting, as sheepishly as a six-foot-three incher weighing 120-odd kilos could, that he had not quite bothered looking up Indian geography till he landed an assignment with the national ruggers.

The waves ravaging Mumbai's Marine Drive were soon eavesdropping on an animated account narrated by a proud Maori, also India's second Kiwi coach after John Wright.

This is a man who has already managed to nudge the Indian team five spots up the world rankings and clinch two wins from five matches since taking over. The team's performance in the World Cup qualifiers in June took them from ninety-one to eighty-six. And this comes after the fifteen straight losses that preceded his appointment.

While touring with a regional Maori team in Switzerland in 2003, Hetaraka was approached by an Indian Rugby Federation official. At first, he gulped at the prospect. Tendulkar and the Taj Mahal were all he knew about the country. But despite his reservations, the forty-one-year-old decided to give it a go.

Hetaraka's first month on the job was marked by the horror of witnessing a bomb blast outside his Mumbai hotel and the hilarity of watching a local club player unwittingly tackle his own teammate. The man, who had masterminded the breaking down of the Wallabie forwards for years, was suddenly expected to drill in the how and why of a backward pass.

For Hetaraka, rugby started early in Bombay Hills. A country boy to the core, he often woke up at 3 am and rubbed his eyes red while tuning into the radio to follow the progress of the world-touring All Blacks.

The ten-year-old's glee at receiving shining rugby boots vanished a day after he jauntered around town in his new pair as his father, a sawmill worker, died of a brief sickness. Hetaraka, the youngest of six, was raised by his mother, who drove a school bus until recently, when she turned seventy.

'But my country gave me a fair opportunity to study at Hamilton Boys School, one of the best places for education and sport alike, and for me, that's the striking difference between India and New Zealand,' says the coach, who, like many foreign hires, doesn't understand why the barriers – socio-economic

Willie Hetaraka: High fives for rugby

and bureaucratic – to sporting success are allowed to exist. 'From the village where I come, I could dream of becoming the PM one day, and mate, we have one chap who managed it.'

The difference is perhaps more glaring for Hetaraka because he bridged the gap – from a small-town, star-struck young rugger to a Maori head coach and national selector – without any conceivable man-devised hassle.

A sprinter and swing-bowler through his school years, Hetaraka played cricket against Martin Crowe and accompanied former Kiwi opener Mark Greatbatch during a New Zealand Schools' Second's rugby tour. All this with minimum struggle, save the hard yards expected from a sportsman.

A flared-up Achilles heel cut short his All Blacks aspirations, but his professional duties as a cop with the Kiwi police force were as eventful as any could have been. 'We once reached a brawl site straight from game practice, and the offenders froze when we loosened pistols from holsters hanging from our rugby gear,' Hetaraka recalls, as the curved lines on his huge face rearrange into a childlike grin.

Spotting a taxi, he recalls, between cackles of lamely suppressed laughter, how he and two of India's bulkiest rugby forwards packed a cabbie into the boot and drove around town, before struggling out with two sets of catches in four necks, thanks to the cramped arrangement.

A twitching neck is the least of a rugby No. 6's troubles, and Hetaraka, who entered countless scrums as a blindside flanker in his playing days, says Maoris are proud of their scars. 'You learn to get up after being knocked around; it's like climbing a tree – you might trip, but that won't stop you from trying again.'

According to Hetaraka, an Indian sportsperson's biggest affliction is his fragile mind rather than the slight built. 'There's a lack of self-belief in most. So my biggest challenge here was not to train them in tackles; it was to stop them from being intimidated at the international level.'

The other choice in rugby is to get peeled apart. But the tough-talking Kiwi, who spends half his time in Mumbai with the Indian team and the other half coaching the army ruggers, has ensured Indians don't get thrown around.

'He knows how to deal with each player, and with fifteen of us, plus the bench, each essaying different roles, he does it with the ease of a professional,' says Indian forward, Hrishikesh Pendse.

The coach, from rugby's most dominant nation, is known to train with loud, ringing music, mostly a collection of inspirational numbers, and is rarely seen without his massive record player. The Indian Army ruggers have even improvised the haka, incorporating a eulogy to the Himalayas.

Give him two years, says Hetaraka, and he'll get us into the top seventy. 'This is probably the fastest improving team in Asia.'

But more needs to be done, all round. 'Auckland schools alone have thirty AstroTurfs, India has only six or seven. And then you wake up to find

Indian ruggers: The fastest improving team in Asia

New Zealand pushing your hockey team out of the Olympics and wonder how and why,' says Hetaraka, whose daughter Jessica (the second of three) proved quite a handful during a recent rugby training session with the Indian Army squad at Ahmednagar.

The sixteen-year-old, says the proud father, absolutely cleaned them up in a push-up contest.

Unlike Indians, says the coach, New Zealanders root for the black jersey, not for a particular individual. But he says he is amazed by what is behind India's national cricket team – the sea of supporters who hoist eleven men to immortality.

As the clouds gather, Hetaraka wonders aloud how far his bunch of fifteen would go, riding a similar wave of support.

'HAVE FUN!' – THE BOSS HAD TOLD ME, AS I SET OFF ON SHORT notice to Bangalore for a tennis tournament in early 2006 – bungling with hurriedly bought tickets, mumbling about no accreditation. He said it at the fag end of all the relevant instructions. And, with as much assurance as a Honda showroom owner would dare, while handing over keys of a brand new silver Civic for a test-drive to a punk. Now, this kind man suspects you might seriously be considering buying the car; he sincerely wants you to enjoy the ride, but cannot imagine you are Schumi-incarnate, pushing full-throttle denting the lean beauty on bumpy roads.

Surely, when they dispatch reporters to touring events, bosses have good stories and general deference to deadlines in mind – not breezy evenings spent enriching your own tennis experience, gossiping about Sania Mirza's nose-ring on the side, and a no-story, which could be the reporter's idea of fun?

Sports editors can't possibly mean it, when they say 'Have fun!' But then – they do.

This editor knew as well as any fine boss would, that every cheerless outing, every half-hearted effort would reflect when printed on the edition. He knew even better that it wasn't the hardships while chasing a potential story that killed the fun – they enhanced the tale, if anything – it was the reticence of involving yourself in storytelling completely that spoiled the game of words.

Sport is a trivial pursuit taken up seriously by its practitioners and their very many followers and by sportswriters who make a living out of it. I took obedience to orders seriously while writing sport. And, decided to have fun.

As a start, I returned from Bangalore with the tale of Sybille Bammer – a tennis-mommy on tour – counter-punching her way up the rankings ladder. She had comprehended way back then what Maria Sharapova meant by dirty looks given to her by Lindsay Davenport's kid, who recently watched the tall Russian decimate his mum.

Later that year, packed off to trace back the journey of Navnath Fartade, the unheralded junior world champion in rifle shooting – there was little merriment at the outset in trudging through Maharashtra's interiors tracking down the returning winner. Not when, an age-old ineptitude at geography resurfaced putting Mumbai at the vertex of the triangle completed by Kolhapur and Beed districts, when a straight line day-long travel was the plan of action.

The road journey in diametric directions undertaken within a three-day deadline aggravated a previous backache. Trouble with sports, and the frequent breakdowns of sportsmen you interview is that you tend to acquire a little more knowledge than the general public about lumbar vertebrae. And you are acutely aware that your own comeback from injury is at best welcomed by half-dozen colleagues at office, not quite applauded by Wimbledon's thousand gushers.

Accompanied by a zealous photographer, who saw as much potential for shots in the floods visiting Maharashtra then, as in the still-elusive shooter's sight-targets, it was one big wading through the excess waters in Kolhapur where Navanath Faratade trains. Besides the irony of the world-winning shooter practising under a leaking roof in a puddle-range at home, there was the revelation of the most indigenous method adopted by the coach to get young shooters started in one of the most sophisticated Olympic disciplines. Rookies held heavy stones, scaled approximately to the rifle in kilos, and with arms stretched out, stood aiming at the target for 30 minutes, getting a feel of the weight.

Then, onto the shooter's native village in Beed – an arid zone, at the same time as Kolhapur was drenched – where Faratade had cultivated sloping land on a hillock, climbing barefoot carrying six-litre water-pots everyday, before turning shooter. The teenager's struggle to ensure his family didn't starve – the sheer effort of climbing up everyday – while I shamelessly panted doing the same in triple the time, silenced the muttering over the back-niggle.

A juxtaposition with another young boy from the same district who'd been found out for his terror-links, made it to the pages and rounded off the tale. Sporting talent in India could rarely be viewed in isolation of performances. It always went beyond speed, strength and endurance.

Much to the chagrin of friends and relations who believe I get to hobnob with Ganguly and Dravid as a matter of routine and can get them passes for the next game at Wankhede, I don't usually write on cricket. No principled opposition to the game – none that would draw me into an intelligent debate. Just that with priorities like – fun-seeking – my crack at this profession has turned out this way.

I do basketball and squash and sailing and kabaddi and rugby. Rugby gave me my first pat on the back from a resident editor who encouraged rookies to flap around at storytelling – both in content and style – and also earned me his whiff of trust with feature-stories in the future. This, just a day after I'd proved my ungainly command over page-making and Quark Express.

Rugby gave me my first Sunday cover too. And these things tend to matter lots – they reinforce the fun-seeking quest.

But that apart, rugby gave me the first glimpse of sport in its physical extremity. Boxing had me hooked previously. But I was suitably impressed after watching ruggers on a shoddy, uneven field throwing themselves and others around the dusty ground, in stark contrast to the adjoining prim green expanse used for cricket; the grass blades not greatly disturbed by the happenings on the ground.

At around the time when a men's brand of fairness cream was being thrown at Indians, training them in a muddied sport, not to mention the bruises and broken bones, seemed like a challenge a Maori from New Zealand could take up. Big Willie Hetaraka, the coach from the land of the world-champion All Blacks, arrived and boomed that it was fragile minds, rather than frail bodies that posed the real stumbling block for Indians to take to contact sport. The doubts subsided soon enough. At least for the New Zealander's immediate charges who picked up a few international wins, inched ahead in rankings – in the face of the fair and handsome onslaught.

When the current national rugby champions, Indian Army, play games, they present a fine haka (war-dance) – the Maori legacy carried forward, well after the coach's departure. But the tale was as much about the man attempting to battle-harden our boys as it was about India's acceptance of rough regimens in a sport that could reveal the depth of character. Even without recycling Rahul Bose's rugby credentials!

Curiously, the British had introduced both cricket and rugby to Kolkatan clubs 150 years ago. The square-cut caught the fancy more than the back-pass – or was it the aloofness of cricket's playing actions being more acceptable than rugby's enforced contact-touch? Be that as it may, but it's the refugee-Armenian community in Kolkata which is now leading rugby's resurgence in the eastern metropolis – a complex tale of acquired grit in a foreign land, a simple tale of school boys having fun.

The emergence of small-town cricket stars in India will undoubtedly remain the most inspiring sporting story of the decade. Other sports too are finding their top performers in remote interiors. In a village hidden inside Nanded district, a bunch of children from an orphanage had marked the Maharashtra-Andhra border as a finishing-line for their twice-a-week 21 kilometre mileage run in preparation of a career in marathons.

Not much of a career if you consider that the incentive for these teenagers from the Sagroli hamlet was a paper-chit which their coach exchanged for a Rs 50 note if they met ambitious time-targets to complete the run. Not that India's elite runners do significantly better, going by their remunerations. But marathon thrives in Africa's Rift Valley – where Kenyans run their way out of poverty, run to beat deprivation. Budhia might have ended up in caricature as a blatant case of exploitation, but there's no denying that India's rural-scape will yield sturdy athletes as we seek to consolidate our sporting-base (read the mother-discipline of athletics) in the future. The city-folk are too busy hooked to the Internet or watching sports relayed to them on television. Or like me, putting words for action, having fun.

Sedentary lifestyles though, can throw up yet another form of sporting pros. Bridge is dead passive, but it figures on sports pages, and is replete with characters, who enliven a sporting form – they tell the story, live the tale. My grandmother – a strict foot-ruler wielding school teacher in her middle-age years – has kept her mind sharp, her heart stern, playing this card-game. The index figure which would've forced algebra and history to penetrate the most dimwitted heads, often touches the side of the forehead repeatedly to indicate her mastery over the intricately intelligent game, which I can't seem to grapple.

Mumbai witnesses a mixed bag of active bureaucrats and celebrities – at that time, on a break from the partying circuit – assemble every six months for two prestigious bridge tournaments. The proceedings pan out in pin-drop silence, the players' brows if lifted, emanate cold stares to intruders with mundane things like stories on their mind. Outwitting happens with a twitching wicked smile, and there's plenty of guile to spin a monster-spider's palace. No pumping fists in this game played by seasoned professionals, bridge is targeting India's most brain-rich institutions – the IITs – to take the lead in the next generation. The fun-facts to emerge from this interaction: a world champion once failed to notice Sophia Lauren walking past him as he plotted at the bridge table. And unlike chess, a computer is yet to best a human at this psychological puzzle.

Of greater amazement to my mind was kabaddi's attempts at going international. The traditional sport taken up recently and fervently by the British armed forces – because it simulates ambush situations, hence improves reaction-time – finds itself in an incomparable situation where Indians as rule-makers will determine the future trajectory of the sport. Also, challenge their own dominance.

There is of course Sunil Gavaskar who used to head ICC's technical committee and was involved in the tweaking of rules to make cricket friendlier for viewers. But as the originators of Hu Tu Tu, Indians have been innovating with the sport over the last few years – introducing the mat to suit the Japanese, incorporating the shoes to woo the Europeans. All the while staring at the prospect that our strong bastion may well be raided by the Japanese or Iranians who'd prove to be more adept at the modern-mat form of the sport.

Hearing the chief innovator bubble excitedly with talk of additions to the game which would make life easier for rivals was akin to listening to Dr Frankenstein describe the fleshing out of the monster. But it was only sport. And this tactical retreat, so to speak, could well shake up India's own complacent standards.

Shaking up my interpretation of relaxed sports writing and fun is the boss in Mumbai. Me – I could have sat in office, pondered on Sania Mirza's Grand Slam performance next year, gossiped about the intrigues within the cricket team and happily written on neither. But the sports head here persists in sowing the seeds of the story, so to speak. Typically, plenty of effort goes into getting this sapling to agree to branch out, seek the sun, to grow.

Most stories are ideas he picks discerningly from faxed-paper and releases. Brainstorming would sound like the mighty, corporate word for what follows. Simply put, I find ten reasons to paint the proposed story a no-story. A bit of dialectics – not quite Socrates and Marx at work, but a regular feature of every press-room, I'd suppose – resolves the brief for the next day's assignment. Chasing the story after that and tapping it away on the computer, invariably ends up being fun.

Unlike the news and general desks, sport, as a newspaper beat, requires you to partake in both the story-gathering and the page-production. Either of which can appear to be a burden on off-colour days. The thrill of being part of the team though comes in moments when the quietest guy on the desk overhears the day's peppy story discussed at large, grasps its essence, and comes up with a witty headline, that would suddenly lift the flier even higher. A colleague's composed approach to all stories breaking, the creativity in times of chaos – with no pretence of doing anything earth-shattering – is the high for a sports desk girl.

The trappings of such a job are to be found on days when a multinational aligns itself to the Olympic movement, ropes in the stars and studs at glitzy press conferences, and you return having opted for the blueberry cheesecake over a Dutch truffle in the lavish spread at lunch. Such stories rarely go beyond the first run. On simpler, happier days, there's always the newspaper-wrapped 'Sundal mixture' at basketball courts in Chennai's

T Nagar, or the shrunken peanuts called 'beej' offered to you by score-keepers, as hoopsters bounce away at Mumbai's Nagpada neighbourhood to add the joy to famished evenings spent watching cagers fly away in their chosen sport.

'Who reads about all this, in these days of multi-million cricket and motorsport deals?' I often get asked. 'Who doesn't?' is my stock answer. If nothing else, I've had my fun.

SYED **NAZAKAT**

Syed Nazakat, 32, is Assistant News Editor, Asia News Network, Bangkok.

**THE AWARD WINNER**
REGIONAL AWARD, JAMMU AND KASHMIR, PRINT

## 'WITHIN ONE MINUTE MY LIFE WAS IN RUINS'

SYED NAZAKAT VISITS THE VILLAGES NEAR LOC AFTER THE EARTHQUAKE SHOOK THE MOUNTAIN REGION OF KASHMIR ON 8 OCTOBER 2005. DEVASTATED AND HAVING LOST ALL HOPE OF AID FROM THE GOVERNMENT, THE POOR PEOPLE HELP EACH OTHER REBUILD THEIR VILLAGE, THEIR LIVES.

## 'WITHIN ONE MINUTE MY LIFE WAS IN RUINS'

IT IS EARLY AFTERNOON IN THIS REMOTE HAMLET WHICH IS forever poised on the threshold of history and tragedy. Mist still hangs in the air. The men are gathered in the village square. Roshan Bee is seated on the rooftop of what remains of her house.

Coughing and wincing in pain, Roshan Bee walks along the grass track, between her neighbours' reconstructed shack and rubbles of her crumbled house. Her eyes foretell no good days ahead. In her eyes is reflected the tragedy of the people devastated by the 8 October 2005 earthquake. We also see in those darting eyes a rare resilience peculiar to mountain people.

In this village which houses 230 families, 30 people died and 78 were injured in the earthquake.

As a weak winter sun fights a losing battle with the freezing cold, Roshan Bee and her fourteen-year-old son Mohamed Akhtar, are still busy clearing the debris of their house. They are homeless like 945 other residents of this village which lies right on the LoC in Uri sector at 7,500 feet above sea level. She has given up waiting for aid, choosing instead to rebuild her own house.

'We know it is impossible to rebuild our home this winter, but we want to rebuild it as early as possible,' says Roshan Bee standing in the rubble near a hoarding that reads, 'God helps those who help themselves'.

Bee and the others here will need divine intervention. Her face is creased with grief from the death of her elder son – Mohamed Ashraf, just twenty-two, the only bread earner of the family – and her one-month-old grandson Yasir who died in the 8 October quake.

'I don't even have their photographs,' she says while digging up the rubble.

Roshan Bee has never known a happy day, except perhaps the day of her wedding or her elder son's wedding. None of these happy events lasted long. In these parts only the dark days last forever. Her husband died just six years after their wedding, leaving behind three small children. Now, her twenty-two-year-old son has died in the quake just one year after his marriage. 'He (Mohamed Ashraf) was the first from the village to go for a government job. He was a teacher,' she says adding that she received heaps of marriage proposals for him.

She stopped, then continued, 'But within one minute my whole life was in ruins'.

In the village it is not difficult to spot the families who have lost their loved ones. The whole village is dotted with red flags, signifying the loss of human life and yellow flags, signifying the loss of livestock. Churunda, high

In these mountanious regions of Jammu and Kashmir, survival is an everyday battle

above Uri town, atop the desolate mountains overlooking Haji Pir area of Pakistan, is as impossible a place as any can be. The Arctic would seem a better choice. The wind is always howling as if mocking the few residents there and the snow comes in savage quantities. There is no shop in the village and Uri, some 26 kilometres away, is the nearest market town. And when the village is buried under snow it will remain isolated till April the next year.

For Roshan Bee and others who live in the mountains, survival will be more difficult. The only sign of the government here is a primary school just reopened a fortnight after it was destroyed in the quake. The army has restored the electricity in the village. But the Himalayan winter has already delivered its opening blitz for over 75,000 homeless families across earthquake-hit regions in J&K and it is freezing.

Like many other quake-hit hilly remote villages, this one has had this season's first snowfall, about one and half feet. But it melted within days. Just a few glistening patches of icy powder remained on the slopes. This marks the start of a potentially deadly four-month season for quake survivors. The reprieve is alarmingly temporary.

The night temperature has already dropped to as low as -10 degrees centigrade. Being a remote village this means that the NGOs and government officials will never make it here. There is no road network and many relief workers are also saying that there is now a restriction on movement in the villages which lie very close to the border, making transportation to and from most of them, impossible. Three doctors, one a woman, came here two days after the quake and since then no doctor has visited the village.

Families usually stock grain, fuel, and other essential commodities for the period that they are cut off. This year, with family stocks decimated and very little cash in hand, no one is sure how Bee and others in the village will survive the winter.

I asked Bee why she can't leave the place before it starts snowing. 'My roots are here. I don't want to live in refugee camps where you are at the mercy of others,' she replies bluntly.

Bee has to finish her work quickly, because her eleven-year-old youngest son Aslam, a class sixth student will be returning home from the primary school, hungry. The school has reopened just a fortnight after it was destroyed in the quake. It is the last working day at school before it closes for the two-month long winter vacation.

'I have to prepare food for him,' Bee explains. She stops for a while and then continues, 'We just have a 30 kilo rice bag and dal in our home.'

The tragedy of Roshan Bee is that while she is facing hard times here, she has no news about her two brothers who migrated to PoK in the early nineties like twenty-seven other families of this small village.

'I just want to see my brothers and their families,' she says.

Her hope that she would see her brothers again was rekindled, last month, when India and Pakistan agreed to open the LoC just below her

Living in refugee camps at the mercy of others

Roshan Bee: Waiting for divine intervention

village. But to her disappointment the LoC was opened only for the exchange of relief.

It is very hard to tell which area belongs to Pakistan and which to India. The only thing which divided this village from Pakistan is the Uri rivulet or what Pakistan calls Hajipeer nallah, which remains dry most of the time.

Further away from Roshan Bee's destroyed house, a fire is kindled, bodies huddle close to it. This is Beebee Jan, forty-two, Roshan Bee's neighbour who has also lost her eighteen-year-old daughter, Manshe, in the quake. Despite being very close, Roshan Bee hardly used to talk with Beebee Jan before the quake. In remote hamlets, residents strangely keep to themselves. But now the quake has transformed them and they have started to communicate with each other. Roshan Bee has become very close to Beebee Jan after the quake. 'We have become just like sisters,' says Roshan Bee. 'We have meals together, we cry together. She tells me what is happening to her and I tell her what is happening to me,' adds Beebee Jan.

'You know, we see just hardship in our lives and we are afraid of what our children will see,' says Beebee Jan, sobbing uncontrollably.

It is easy to be a cynic here.

In the past fifty years or more, this village at the edge of LoC, has been soaked in blood. In 1947, tribal invaders plundered the village which was divided in two parts by the LoC. Then came the India-Pakistan border tensions and artillery shelling. Then in 2003, the village got fenced out from the rest of the country. For the last two-and-half years the people were enjoying a bit of peace and freedom after a cease fire between India and Pakistan. That was before the earthquake left this village totally in rubble. Needless to say, tragedy and death are frequent visitors here.

As dusk gathers, the village square is quiet. Children and women sit in the doorways of their destroyed homes clad in donated clothes, their only possession. Roshan Bee carries wood logs to her tent. She is joined by her sons, Akhtar, and then Aslam, and then by Beebee Jan. As we leave the village, melodic flute music resounds from some part of the village.

Tomorrow will be another day of work and survival.

ONE OF MY EARLIEST, AND RECURRING NIGHTMARE IS ABOUT being trapped in a gunbattle between the troops and militants in Kashmir. The air is filled with gunshots and cries. People run in every direction, stooping below the smoke, screaming. The sound of bullets comes closer and closer – I am frozen to the spot, staring – and trying to turn and run. I can see people all around me in a pool of blood. Dead. The encounter intensifies and I hear a strange thunderous sound from somewhere, a sound I have never heard before. But somebody just takes me away seconds before the bullets hit me.

Where did my childhood dream come from?

A psychologist might say it showed my fear of being overwhelmed by emotions. I was born in Srinagar, Kashmir, so my first memory is of running away with my brother every time there was a gun battle between militants and the troops. We used to run to save our lives from the fire and rampage. I was just a ten-year-old boy when armed insurgency started in Kashmir in 1989. Since then life in the Kashmir Valley revolves around killings and tragedies.

But later when I joined journalism it was always the other way around. Instead of running away from killings and tragedies I saw myself often chasing the bloody gun battles to reach the killing spots. There was always this curiosity to get closer to the story, to spot, to death. I remember when I first saw the bullet-ridden bodies. I cried. But years later I found myself unable to mourn death and tragedies. One more death was just another story.

Tragedies and disasters are always most touching and chilling when you know the terrain and the people. When the earth opened its jaws of death in Kashmir on 8 October 2005 it was emotionally stressful to cover the earthquake. It was tough to get stories out of the quake survivors, to let the outside world understand how a killer quake has changed their lives forever. The earthquake had destroyed mosques, Hindu temples, gurudwaras, and churches with indiscriminate violence. It had swept away everything. It had killed people of almost every religion and those without one. It seemed God was angry and had a mission to destroy.

Three years after the powerful earthquake, it is not yet easy to comprehend or analyse the causes and consequences of the colossal tragedy. In Pakistan-occupied Kashmir, over 73,000 people were killed, 70,000 people were severely injured or disabled and three million people were left homeless. The Indian side of Kashmir also reported heavy casualties with over 1,300 people dead, 6,622 injured and over two lakh people left homeless in the immediate aftermath of the quake.

I was at my apartment in South Delhi when the earthquake hit Kashmir.

My editor called up and said that I should go to cover the earthquake. I left Delhi and went to Kashmir. When I reached Srinagar airport everything seemed almost normal: armoured cars, check points and flak-jacketed soldiers dotting the roads. There were tourists hunting for taxis under a sun glinting off mountain peaks. I asked my driver about the earthquake. 'It was terrible,' he said, 'but thank God we survived.'

Instead of staying in Srinagar, we decided to go to Uri, a border town at the LoC that divides Kashmir into two parts – Indian Kashmir and Pakistani Kashmir. We entered Uri at around 10 pm and stopped at a roadside shop. Everywhere there was death and destruction. Homes had been reduced to rubble. Villagers were braving the numbing cold and hunger. The roads were blocked and the only way to reach the devastated and remote villages of Uri was to travel by narrow landslide-prone damaged roads and then walk on foot.

I walked past the destroyed houses, unable to comprehend the scale of the tragedy. The hills were dotted with houses destroyed by the quake and there were many villages, completely wiped off the face of earth. Atop of the mountain in Mardyaan village, dozens of people were lying dead with no one to even pick them up. Vultures had begun circling above the village.

Those were horrible days in Uri.

The people were at loss to understand what had happened to them. So many people were dead, but what did their deaths mean – except that our earth is fragile to the core and that nobody and no one can escape its power? Some of the dead could have been militants, used to cross-border infiltration, killings, and bombings. But they would have perished, too, like the Indian and Pakistani troops atop of the mountains guarding the frontline, the kids in the streets, the politicians in their offices, the devotees at prayers – all common victims of the natural disaster.

Disaster often becomes a moral bellwether for the people, the nation: how much do we actually care? That is why humanity often flourishes in the face of human tragedies. So it was not a surprise that I saw soldiers of India and Pakistan leaving their guns on the ground and joining hands to rescue people and reconstruct roads. I met a young army doctor at the army hospital in Uri. Dr Saurabh Dawra who had just flown in from his home in Chandigarh to help people he hardly knew. He, like other army doctors, was working round the clock to save the lives of injured people. There were hundreds and hundreds of people from Srinagar city with loads of relief material reaching out to the remote inaccessible border villages to help survivors.

But the massive Kashmir earthquake did not attract sustained press coverage. The quake had almost fallen off the news agenda of international and national media – and the UN reported a poor response to its emergency appeal. The indifference in media coverage made a real and tangible difference to people's lives. The extensive press coverage of the tsunami helped the UN to raise 80 per cent of its appeal for emergency aid in just ten days. But the international media failed to provide sustained coverage to the Kashmir earthquake. With little help coming from outside, Pakistan struggled in the initial days to cope with the situation.

In India, unfortunately, some TV channels covered the earthquake in such a way that gave the impression that the earthquake had just struck the other side of Kashmir, the Pakistani side. They preferred to highlight stories that described the destruction of militant camps in Muzaffarabad in an almost jubilant tone, perhaps with the result that there was a kind of indifference to the suffering of people in Kashmir.

During my first visit to Kashmir immediately after the quake there was almost no help from outside the Valley. Whatever help came was from the local people within the Valley. The public response in the rest of country to the Kashmir earthquake was in total contrast with what we had seen during the Gujarat earthquake in 2001 when people across the country came forward to help the quake survivors.

Perhaps editors, fresh from covering the tsunami, were also suffering from 'compassion fatigue'. They had an idea that the public is not interested in seeing people dying. But I was fortunate that my editors funded my frequent travels to cover the earthquake. We at *Sahara Times* were amongst the few news organisations that followed the story many months after the earthquake. I remember when I went to Kashmir in April 2006 to do follow-up stories on the quake, there was hardly any coverage in the national media.

Even in the initial days of the quake what you mostly missed from the coverage of the earthquake was a sense of the people, the suffering of the border people. Immediately after the earthquake, the defence ministry allowed people including journalists and relief workers to walk freely in the border areas. It was for the first time the border areas were thrown open to the rest of the world. The LoC is one of the most heavily militarised borders in the world where India and Pakistan have fought two wars and their troops are still in eyeball-to-eyeball contact. The villages all along the 720-kilometre long LoC are a land of jungles and mountain, of brutal fortresses and killing fields, of border enmity and bloodshed. Every border village gives you a sense of siege as there are more troops than local people. And despite a durable ceasefire between India and Pakistan in the last few years, the sufferings of border people have not ended.

Imagine an old woman climbing about 6,000 ft up a hill from her village, descending 6,000 ft on the other side, just to buy some food for her family and then climbing back up that mountain of 6,000 ft to the top of the hill, descending the same distance to return to her village. This is a real-life story missed by media, unintentional or deliberately, and one of perhaps tens of thousands distressing stories that are unfolding in the border areas of Kashmir every day.

As if that was not enough, the border fencing brought more hardships to the people. The fence, intertwined with concertina wire, is India's effort to keep out what it says are terrorists trained and backed by Pakistan to wrest control of Kashmir. But the fencing of the 720-kilometre-long LoC has left thousands of people in an awkward situation.

The fence should actually have come up on the LoC but Pakistani shelling had forced the Indian Army to move the fence a little inside Indian territory leaving some villages on the wrong side of the fence. Pakistan had objected to the fencing, saying LoC is not demarcated so border fencing cannot be done. As a result, villagers who are caught on the wrong side of fence, wonder which place they belong to – India, Pakistan or No Man's Land.

There is no transport to the village. To approach it, the villagers have to walk past the Mike post, the last Indian Army camp on this side of the LoC in southern Uri sector. Then they climb the snow-clad slope up the final seven kilometres to Churunda. The nearest market is 26 kilometre away. At night villagers are literally cut off from the outside world as the security forces lock the only entry point, a steel gate on the partition fence which remains open for only eight hours a day. The villagers need permission from the army to go to the grocery store, to visit the family and to attend a wedding or even funeral in the nearby village.

In Chandura, it is hard to tell which area belongs to Pakistan and which to India. The only thing that divides this village into two parts is the Uri rivulet or what Pakistan calls Hajipeer nallah. It is dry most of the time. Before India and Pakistan fought a war following the violent division of the subcontinent in 1947, the people who lived on both sides were kinfolk and friends. They spoke the same tongue. They ate the same chapattis. They still speak the same language and break the same bread, though they are now citizens of two 'enemy' nations. Only birds, like the black partridge native to this land, can fly freely over the border.

Legendary writer Saadat Hasan Manto has captured the misery of the border people of Kashmir in his moving story 'The Dog of Tetwal'. The story revolves around Indian and Pakistani soldiers at Tetwal post at the LoC who play a strange game with a stray dog as he runs from this side of border to that side, with each side claiming ownership. Eventually the dog is fired at by soldiers on both sides and dies 'a dog's death', as the story concludes.

The people living in border areas, like the dog of Tetwal, are suffering the same fate for the last fifty years.

Three years later, as I sit here in my lit-up room, barricaded with papers and books, I think about the earthquake survivors I had left behind at Uri and Tangdar. Just three years after the quake, and I can barely remember how terrible the earthquake was.

The reporter in me wants to go back and see how Roshan Bee is doing. Has she managed to rebuild her destroyed house? I want to meet Nazeer Ahmed, the shopkeeper of Uri town, whose shop and house was destroyed in the quake. I want to meet little Pervez who had lost twenty-four relatives to the earthquake. He wanted to play cricket but his left arm was yet to recover from the wounds when I met him in a Srinagar hospital. I want to meet Ulfat and her brothers who had lost both their parents in the quake. I want to go to Chandura village and see if that border door has opened a little wider.

VIVEK MADHAO **DESHPANDE**

Vivek Madhao Deshpande, 44, is Assistant Editor, Nagpur edition of *The Indian Express*.

**THE AWARD WINNER**
UNCOVERING INDIA INVISIBLE, PRINT

# THE TIP OF TERROR

LAUNCHED TO COUNTER NAXALITES IN THE TRIBAL BELTS OF CHHATTISGARH, HAS THE SALVA JADUM CAMPAIGN TURNED COUNTER-PRODUCTIVE? VIVEK DESHPANDE TRAVELS TO KONTA IN SOUTH BASTAR TO FIND THAT THIS COULD BE JUST THE BEGINNING OF A LONG ARDUOUS JOURNEY.

TUCKED AWAY ON THE SOUTHERN TIP OF CHHATTISGARH where the state's border touches Orissa and Andhra Pradesh, is the once obscure, now frightened tehsil of Konta.

On the way to this terror tip, clusters of ramrod-straight trees rise high up from the famous Abujmad forests, painting a breathtaking skyline against the backdrop of an unending hill range. For about 30-odd kilometre before Konta, it's just another day for the tribals of Bastar.

Then just round the corner a mist of gloom surrounds you stealthily. During the last 30-kilometre journey to Konta, it clings to you jealously, never seeming to let you go.

Then it gives way suddenly. At Konta the mist lifts to expose the desolation. The broken government building and huts are the tell-tale signs of a violent storm. The tension is loud and the terror screaming.

Will peace ever return? That's the question in many minds in this land first ravaged by Naxalism and now haunted by Salva Judum, a 'popular' movement against extreme Left violence. The campaign is government sponsored and backed by the opposition Congress. It first began in the Bijapur-Geedam belt in west Chhattisgarh in June last year and has now spread south as far as Konta. Over 30,000 people have been 'coerced' into deserting their villages and shifting to the twenty heavily guarded 'relief camps' across south Bastar.

Konta camp, is the first in the deep south. Nearly 10,000 paramilitary personnel, reserve policemen, regular state police and NSG commandos have been deployed to protect such camps and secure the transit of the shifting population. Tribal youths recruited as special police officers and armed with guns, bows and arrows and sharp-edged weapons man every entry and exit point.

Nobody knows exactly how many have been killed so far, but the casualty list on both sides could run into hundreds and it's going up by the day. The biggest of the strikes occured when Naxalites blasted a truck carrying Judum participants, killing over twenty-six and injuring over forty others. Incidentally, the landmine was laid more than five years ago – Naxalites have strewn south Bastar with landmines that they can blow up at will whenever required.

## CAUGHT IN THE CROSSFIRE

Chief Minister Raman Singh calls Salva Judum 'a war by harassed tribals against the terror of AK-47 and RDX'; leader of the Opposition in the Assembly, Mahendra Karma calls it 'a war against Naxal violence and

Salva Judum: Fighting Spirit

suppression'. Raman Singh and Karma may be in this together, travelling to remote villages addressing Judum rallies, but in the war against militant leftism, if there is a victim it is the tribal who is caught in the crossfire.

In the chaos of Judum dominated areas, tribals can be seen making their way to camps. Some have joined the revolution of their own volition, other have little choice since the unwritten rule is clear: join the Judum.

The Judum strategy is not complex: explain things to Sangam leaders (Naxal dalams frontmen in villages), then pressurise them. If they still don't agree, beat them up and hand them over to the police. The bottom line is: no is not an answer.

At the camps, the members are supposed to build their own makeshift houses while the government provides them food. Twice a day they queue up for a roll call and a drill.

With the younger men leaving for camps, there are many villages almost entirely left to the women, children and the old. Since the Naxals usually do not harm them, there are no compunctions in leaving them alone.

Back at the camp, a look at the tense faces around and it's hard to believe they have responded spontaneously to the Judum call. There are, however, a few who appear enthusiastic and energised.

## HOMEGROWN TERROR

Whatever their reasons for signing up, everyone at the camps agrees about the 'lack of adequate security' for the Judum campaigners. Revenue officials privately lambast the state police. At Ganglur village – where Naxalites had killed eight Judum supporters one February night after laying siege to the police station– *The Sunday Express* came across relaxed policemen enjoying a game of carrom. Two of them – one dressed as a woman – danced outside the police station to the accompaniment of drumbeats even as villagers watched from a distance.

Beyond the apparent normality, there is so much tension that even journalists are cautioned against venturing into these areas. They have an additional worry. The administration, it seems, is determined to ensure a good press for Judum. Last month the Chhattisgarh Assembly passed a bill that empowers the government to act against any adverse publicity given to Judum. Bijapur superintendent of police, Manhar, was caught in a row when reports appeared in local press about a tape that contained his alleged threat to journalists writing against Judum.

In Konta, a new danger is fast raising its head. As an offshoot of Judum, there is a war between the two different tribes. Dorlas and Muriyas developing there.

And then there is the menace that is the bane of all such armed movements. According to local journalists and traders, Judum activists are now going into overdrive to extort money by arm-twisting and harassing vulnerable people.

Naxalites maintain that the Judum is an uprising orchestrated by the creamy layer tribals like the Patels, Manjhis and Kotwars, 'the repressive traditional tribal community heads and non-tribals whom we have marginalised'.

The truth lies somewhere in between. Looking at many Judum leaders like K Madhukar Rao, the original protagonist who started it at Ambeli village in Bijapur, Naxalites aren't exactly off the mark. Says a non-tribal teacher from a remote village who has watched Naxalism grow in the region: 'What Naxalites did was rob the tribals of their property and distributed it among the poorer. So these people are naturally angry and the Judum leadership is concentrated in their hands.'

A tribal teacher adds the conmen view: 'All this is true but tribals don't want to remain in obscurity forever. They want development and as long as Naxalites are there, the road to development will be shut to them.'

An anti-Judum Naxalite booklet counters these allegations with a question: 'Are all those places where there are roads really developed?' it asks. 'Roads are actually meant for the police,' it adds.

Development is much debated but almost entirely missing in this tribal

Arming the Salva Judum to fight against extreme Left violence

earthland. Residents of remote villages sometimes have to be carried on makeshift stretchers for nearly 25 kilometres to the nearest hospital.

So even those who oppose the Salva Judum campaign agree that Naxal presence will always keep development away. A tribal teacher-cum-activist says, 'Judum is not a spontaneous movement for development. It's coercive. But development is surely everybody's demand.'

Karma seems to be reflecting their viewpoint when he says, 'Ask them (Naxals) what have they done for the tribals during the twenty-five years of their stay there?' How deep the schism is in this region can be gauged by the comment of another Konta resident: 'It's not that the Naxals haven't done any development. They have also constructed water tanks and run schools in deep interiors.'

Yet the common complaint is that Naxalites don't allow people to participate in government programmes and how the tendu leaf collection, the main off-season source of earning for the people, has virtually ended because of Naxalites fleecing the contractors.

But the question everyone is asking is: why did the Naxalites target the tribals if they believe the Judum campaign was not a popular movement and tribals were being forced into joining its ranks?

'It shows they are getting desperate and that they don't really love the tribals,' alleges Karma. 'For them, tribals are mere pawns in their violent pursuit of political power.'

The brave words apart, there is still a big question mark hanging over the future of Salva Judum. 'How long can it pull on?' is an oft-heard refrain among those following the developments closely. 'This is most likely to end in disaster. How long can the government sustain this war?' asks an activist.

The people's movement comes with a danger inherent in its origins. Explains a top police officer from Maharashtra: 'It is extremely dangerous to arm tribal youth. I shudder to think what would happen if they run amok.'

The fear is echoed in other quarters. 'Arming the youth isn't the right way of going about anti-insurgency. It will ultimately prove counter-productive,' said a top retired bureaucrat known for his lasting anti-insurgency work in the Northeast.

Mohan Hirabai Hiralal has come up with a model of tribal self-rule in the Mendha Lekha village in Vidarbha's Naxal-intensive Gadchiroli district. He is unsure about the tribals taking up arms. 'The tribals don't like the campaign. Neither do they like the extremist path. They are always looking for a way that is in tune with their traditional independent democratic structures. We need to resurrect these structures to positively channelise the tribal frustration than do Judum kind of campaigns,' he says.

But is the administration listening? Raman Singh and Karma are determined to take the campaign to its end. 'It is going to be a fight to the finish,' says Karma in the manner of a melodrama producer. '*Ye lambi chalnewali ladaai hai* (this will be a long-drawn battle),' says a more circumspect Singh.

But how long is long-drawn? 'Till the battle is won,' replies Karma promptly. The chief minister says the government plans to create clusters of villages so that a bigger community force can be created to deter the Naxalites. 'These clusters would be suitably located in the forests and will be able to protect themselves from Naxalite violence,' he adds.

But Karma's own party members are now protesting. 'Look at the sorry state of affairs at the camps. And the government is unable to safeguard the lives of tribals,' said a group of twenty Congress MLAs who visited Konta last Thursday.

'Politicisation could eventually prove to be the last nail in Judum's coffin,' warns another local activist.

People protesting against the campaign say that day is not too far off.

IT WAS SOMETIME IN DECEMBER 2005 THAT I WAS SUDDENLY alerted to some extraordinary happenings in the Chhattisgarh state. For a few months, I had been reading a few routinely reported stories about clashes between tribals and Naxalites. It sounded quite strange that the tribals had taken up arms against those who were seen by many as their saviours. The stories, however, had hardly made a buzz outside Chhattisgarh. As a reporter covering Naxalism in the bordering districts of Vidarbha, adjacent to Naxalite-infested Chhattisgarh, Orissa and Andhra Pradesh, I thought the issue needed to be studied in greater detail and its story properly documented. Incidentally, *The Indian Express*, then, had no correspondent in Chhattisgarh. So, I suggested to my Delhi office that we must take this up immediately and that I would like to do it. It was immediately okayed. So, I started working on it. Some police officials from Maharashtra having first-hand experience of anti-Naxalite operations in Vidarbha and a few tribal activists told me that going out there was extremely risky. One of them also told me that a superintendent of police in one of the affected districts had been caught on tape telling his men to bump off journalists giving adverse publicity to the 'tribal uprising' against Naxalites.

But I had often been deep into the Naxalite belt of Maharashtra. Some of the places were in the famous Abujmad liberated zone of the Naxalites where not many journalists are known to have ever gone. At one such place in Maharashtra, I and my photographer Shekhar Soni were virtually held hostage for a few hours by a group of Naxalites, who, before leaving the place, had asked the villagers not to let us go until the next morning. We, however, risked an early exit. So, I thought visiting South Bastar to cover what had by then come to be known as Salva Judum was a risk worth taking.

But the challenge was really difficult, mainly because I had never been to the area and I knew nobody there. Police officials and activists from Maharashtra, however, helped by putting me on to their counterparts there. I finalised the plan by discussing with them all the ifs and buts I needed to sort out the dos and don'ts I needed to know before venturing out into the strife-torn area.

In February 2006, I set out for South Bastar along with photographer Shekhar Soni. By covering 600 kilometres by road in a day, we reached the critical Geedam-Bijapur area where the first Salva Judum spark had been ignited. Along the way, we had stopped at the capital Raipur and had spoken about our mission to the state Publicity Department chief so that nothing was left to suspicion. We also talked a few basic issues out with a few tribal activists before leaving for Bijapur, the biggest town right in the heart of the Salva Judum battlefront. As we reached Geedam, we started getting a sense of what Salva Judum was about. The entire road from Geedam to Bijapur was dotted with boards of Salva Judum slogans. We caught the first glimpse of the Salva Judum relief camp on the way. There was a police picket and even as we stopped our vehicle there, a few policemen and tribal youths approached us. Their probing eyes gave us a good hard look. We had decided not to hide our identities as mediapersons – it would have been counter-productive had it become known at a later stage.

After some preliminary inquiries, we headed straight for Bijapur where we were to meet a few local journalists whom we had sounded out about our arrival from Jagdalpur, the main big town and the district headquarter of Bastar.

It was here that we got a real sense of Salva Judum. A thorough check of our vehicle by tribal youths – boys and girls – trained as Special Police Officers (SPOs) and the prying eyes of the security personnel trained to look at every new arrival in the dusty town with suspicion had us on high alert. The local journalist, Mohammad Yakub, an extremely affable person, took us inside the sprawling Salva Judum camp in Bijapur where we met this controversial 'bump-them-off' SP. The meeting with him only confirmed the impression that we had of him. While we were talking, he suddenly turned to my photographer and asked him why he was hiding behind me. Actually, Shekhar was trying to catch a picture of the camp with the SP and his armed guards in the foreground.

The same day, Yakub took us to Gangalur, a village about 25 kilometre deep inside the inaccessible forests of Bijapur. Bijapur-Gangalur is one of the most dreadful roads in Bastar. It was on this road that Naxalites had blown up an anti-landmine vehicle killing about twenty-seven security personnel in September 2005. And Gangalur was where they had conducted a guerrilla raid on a Salva Judum rally in the dead of night and had killed seven SPOs right near the police station, just ten days before we were there. The Bijapur camp itself was the target of Naxalite ire on many occasions.

As a matter of fact, landmine blasts and sudden attacks were the order of the day in the entire Salva Judum belt. Needless to say, our visit was fraught with many dangers.

In the camps, tension on the people's faces was palpable. One couldn't miss the fact they had been forced into a strife they hadn't started and they didn't really want. With security personnel all around them, they would hardly say anything and would mostly mumble monosyllables. There was no missing the fact that most of them were not happy with the turn of events that had dislodged them from their native villages and had alienated them from their agricultural land and cattle. In their own beautiful land, they had become refugees forced to fight a battle that promised to offer little solace to them.

Next day, we went to Kutru village on the other side of the district. Tucked deep inside the border part of the district and surrounded by thick forest, it was the last place one could reach by a tarred road. Kutru was where K Madhukar Rao, the original Salva Judum protagonist, belonged. A teacher in a nearby village, it was Rao who had first organised a few villages to revolt against Naxalites in June 2005 at the nearby Karkeli village. Unfortunately, he was out, leading the Salva Judum procession to Sipamarka village to 'annex' it to the Judum realm. The Judum procession marched virtually like the mythological Ashwamedh through Bastar Naxalite-controlled interiors, getting the villages to submit to it. A refusal would mean a handover to the police. I wanted to interview Rao at any cost, so I thought I would try and reach Sipamarka, which was about 40 kilometre further into the district. The police strongly advised against going there – there was a dusty village road that went only up to Farsegad beyond which vehicles couldn't travel. But we decided to still give it a try. So, we reached Farsegad, which was the last police outpost on that side, about 18 kilometre from Kutru. We were told that just a week earlier, Naxalites had surrounded the village and had fought a pitched battle with the police and the Salva Judum army. It is here that the boundary of the doomed Indravati Tiger Reserve starts. The local police officer refused to allow us to go to Sipamarka, about 25 kilometre further away, saying the forest along the road was a veritable Naxalite hideout where even the police don't often go. Only the previous night Naxalites had thrown bombs at the Judum procession at Sipamarka. We decided to overrule the officer's directive and started moving towards the place – one thing I was always sure about was there was no getting the real story without taking the risk. Unfortunately, our vehicle got stuck inside a nullah and we had to return to Farsegad where we decided to wait for the Judum procession to return. We were told it could take three to four hours. Till then, we discussed the Judum campaign with the villagers, camp inmates and the SPOs.

Finally, at a distance inside the forest, we could see a huge winding procession marching towards Farsegad, raising a cloud of dust. Just as it came nearer, the shouting of slogans got louder, breaking the eerie calm that had enveloped the forest village till then. Shekhar was excited – it was indeed a rare photo-opportunity. When the procession came within close range, it provided an awesome spectacle. An army of thousands of tribal men and women, carrying their baggage on the back and wielding sharp weapons, bows and arrows and sticks in hands, marched in unison even as security personnel wielding firearms marched in rows on both the sides providing an impregnable security cordon. K Madhukar Rao was leading the procession. And as it turned out, we were the first to catch a snap shot of a Salva Judum procession, which got splashed on the front page of *The Sunday Express* on February 26 when we carried the first of the several reports on the issue published through the year.

I had a long, interesting interview with Rao, a fearless man who had the guts to take on the mighty and tricky Naxalites in their own bastion. Inherent flaws in a campaign like Judum notwithstanding, Rao and his followers' resolve was too bold to be dismissed outright.

By the time we finished our work, it was already getting dark and we needed to leave quickly since it wasn't advisable to travel in the area during night. When we were about to leave, some Judum rallyists asked us to drop them to Kutru. We were apprehensive, since they were all armed and their being in the vehicle meant a huge risk. Incidentally, a year after we were there, Naxalites killed over fifty-five cops and SPOs in a night-long raid at Rani Bodli police outpost along this road.

For the rallyists, however, there was no taking a 'no' for an answer – they just got inside the vehicle leaving no scope for us to say no. Nothing untoward, however, happened and we safely reached Kutru.

The experience only made us tougher and bolder. In our subsequent trips to the region, we encountered other such risks but they hardly worried us.

When we returned to Bijapur, it was already pitch dark. Our journalist friend Yakub advised us to stay back for the night, but we were scheduled to return to Jagdalpur the same day, so again we took the risk of travelling in the dark. En route, we saw hardly any vehicular movement on the 150 kilometre road.

Next day, we returned to Raipur, on the way talking to a few other activists who had been watching the Judum phenomenon closely. In Raipur, I also interviewed Chief Minister Raman Singh and the fiery Opposition leader Mahendra Karma of the Congress, himself a tribal, who had joined hands with the government in the anti-insurgency operation. After three days of a hectic and risky probe, our job was done. We had come out safely, but not without experiencing how perilous it could get out there.

Finally, it was all worth it. When *The Sunday Express* carried the story as page one lead, we were the first to tell the Salva Judum story to the world. Our report brought to the fore the fact that with over 700 deaths in less than two years, Chhattisgarh, and not Kashmir or Northeast, was India's biggest strife-torn area.

Within a week, I had to return to the southern Konta area of Bastar where a landmine blast had killed some twenty-seven Judum rallyists near Darbhaguda. The Judum campaign was predictably getting bloodier and more dangerous.

By this time, I had made a lot of contacts in the region who helped me a lot in unravelling the Judum intricacies.

In July, I had to return once again to cover a massive attack by Naxal militia on the Errabor Judum camp in which over thirty people were killed. Here, we were told how the campaign was running into a self-defeating conflict, pitching the tribals against each other in a fratricidal war that the government and the Naxalites, ironically, were projecting as a fight for justice for them.

I would also like to specifically mention that one of the most important stories in the series was about the huge environmental damage caused by massive tree-felling along the roads where Judum camps came up. This was done to provide clear visibility on both sides of the roads to prevent attacks on Judum camps. In naked violation of the Forest Conservation Act, Judum activists, fully backed by the state government, had cut lakhs of trees even as the forest authorities preferred to turn a Nelson's eye.

We also reported the recruitment of children into Naxal militia, a fact that was subsequently confirmed by Intelligence agencies.

## THROWING THE LIGHT OF TRUTH

As a journalist, I had often ventured out into danger zones, be it the Naxalite area, a communal riot or a Vidarbha forest inhabited by a man-eater tiger. That, I believe, is not very difficult. The real challenge, I feel, lies in telling the story with the appropriate perspective. Since you are the lone representative of your paper to witness events of such enormous magnitude and consequences, you have to get not only every fact and figure correct, but also the entire perspective on the issue right. That is all the more so if you happen to be breaking the story, because others follow you and get to verify what you have written. And, in the end, it goes as your paper's take on the issue. So, not only is your own credibility at stake but also that of your newspaper. That's why the real challenge before a one-man bureau lies in telling the story that will never ever fly in the face of actual ground realities.

As always, here too, the most important consideration that weighed on my mind was that I must remain objective at any cost. And to achieve objectivity, the cardinal principle of journalism, inarguably, is to tell how anything that one reports about affects the people at large.

The principle applies particularly to issues such as Naxalism. Because on one hand, there is a crude understanding about Naxalism as a law and order problem and, on the other, there is a rather romantic perception about how the 'movement' is fighting for and on behalf of the poor and the underprivileged. Journalism can give one bouts of activism. The thumb-rule to avoid them is to know that truth doesn't necessarily lie on any one side. In my career spanning twenty years, fifteen of them with *The Indian Express*, I have always tried to stick to this principle. Even in my reporting on Vidarbha's agrarian crisis, which incidentally came to light after my 2002 story on the spate of farmers' suicides sweeping the region, I rarely did suicide numbers as the main story of the crisis, because while it was true that agrarian crisis had made life difficult for farmers, the activistic tendency to highlight every suicide in the countryside as agrarian suicide amounted to sensationalising the issue. And suicide numbers are not the real index of the crisis. So, to bust these fantastic claims, we dared to swim against the current by doing a story about how most of the suicides being reported as suicides for farm reasons had actually nothing to do with agriculture. That attracted a lot of jeers from people with vested interests and activists, but we knew we had told nothing but truth.

Again, the telling-of-truth approach applies better to Naxalism and the state's war against it than to most other issues. The driving thought behind doing the Judum series in a particular way was that any anti-Naxalite operation must necessarily aim at drawing the people away from Naxalism by taking the benefits of development to their doorsteps and not by using them as weapons and shields to outwit the Naxalites in an armed conflict as is being done in Salva Judum.

That's why the focus of my Salva Judum stories was the angst of the people, not how the two sides – Naxalites and the government – were faring in the war. I mainly focused on what it meant to the people to be uprooted from their villages and stuffed in the Judum camps. I could see how the poor people lived a tense life in the camps with the sword of a possible Naxal attack constantly hanging over their heads. Most of them were not ready to speak out about how they felt on being dragged into the conflict for obvious reasons. So, even if there was anything in my reports that seemed like a view – for example, how Judum was heading towards a self-defeating zone, it was only a reflection of the ground realities and wasn't something that either sought to purposely villify one side or help fortify the other side's position. At the cost of repetition, I would like to say a journalist must tell the truth that matters to people at large.

My reporting of Salva Judum was, in a sense, vindicated when the Supreme Court, in its observation about Salva Judum on 31 March 2008, said the state can't arm its citizens to fight a war. It was more of a legal point, which, frankly, didn't strike me when I was reporting the matter. I think the arming of citizens is only the façade of Salva Judum. It is actually more about using them as shields and weapons in a conflict that the state should ideally fight on its own, if at all it has to be fought with arms.

Reporters from across the world later followed the *Express* Judum story. The series was also short-listed for the Kurt Schork Award for international journalism. And it later won the Ramnath Goenka Award. I was happy about the honour, but that my reports first decoded the Judum phenomenon and the dreadful realities of the intense fratricidal strife in Bastar gave me the inner satisfaction every journalist longs for.

ZAFFAR **IQBAL**

Zaffar Iqbal, 36, is Principal Correspondent with NDTV.

**THE AWARD WINNER**
REGIONAL AWARD, J&K, BROADCAST

## JOURNALISM IN KASHMIR

IN THE CONTEXT OF A TERRIFYING BRUSH WITH VIOLENCE AND TURMOIL IN SRINAGAR, ZAFFAR IQBAL RELATES HIS FEELINGS FOR HIS OWN PEOPLE AND HIS SENSE OF EMPATHY FOR THEM.

JOURNALISM IN VIOLENT JAMMU-KASHMIR IS TOUGH. JOURNALISTS do not get many opportunities to do positive stories, and the reporting mostly hinges on violence and tragedies. But covering that almost on a daily basis can also make a journalist insensitive to the situation and the people involved in it. Sometimes the greatest tragedies are reduced to mere numbers while working in a deadline atmosphere of journalism.

My journalistic career in Jammu-Kashmir saw me cover many tragic events, but I have also done stories of hope and optimism. The story on 'Kashmiri Models' was just one of them. Being brought up in an atmosphere of violence and turmoil in Srinagar has helped me relate more easily to stories about the problems of the youth in Jammu-Kashmir and their aspirations.

Of all the experiences, this one was the most important.

In 2002, after completing my masters in Mass Communication and Journalism, I started working as a reporter for a local daily in Srinagar. On 29 May 2002, I reached the office around noon after covering a press conference and started filing my story. Just then, Narayan, the office boy entered the newsroom and told me that some people had come to the office and wanted to meet me. I left my story halfway, thinking it might be something important, not realising who they were or the nature of their mission.

They were three men in their twenties, posing as courier agents and they said they had come to deliver a letter. I talked with them for a few minutes while they were shuffling the letters in their bag. We spoke of their qualifications, the location of their office and other such matters. It was a very calm conversation. But when they handed me the letter and I had signed their register and was about to turn back, I could not believe my eyes: one of them took out a gun, he had been hiding till then, and thrust it to my head and shot at point blank range. For a moment, I did not realise what had happened, but in a split second it was clear to me that this was a militant attack by the men who had come in the guise of courier agents and I was the victim of mistaken identity. My world came crashing down. I thought that my life was about to end. The bullet broke my skull and came out from the root of the nose, fracturing it, before hitting the wall. I noticed blood trickling down my face. It was a small trickle at first and then became a stream of blood in no time. As I tried my best to move away from that place, they kept shooting at me, indiscriminately; two more bullets hit me on both my legs. Many bullets missed me. Finally, I ended up in a pool of blood – it was all over, I thought. The assassins escaped, nobody caught them. I did not lose consciousness, kept my calm and prayed to God. That gave me a lot of strength at the time. I had survived. I felt there was some strange, invisible and powerful force at work at the time.

After the shoot-out, there was complete silence in the room for a few minutes, but that silence was broken when my colleagues from the newsroom reached the spot. Asif was the first one to reach me, then the others. They first tried to stop the bleeding with their handkerchiefs. When that failed, they tried to stop it with window curtains and everything they could lay their hands on. Finally, they rushed me to the Government Medical College Hospital of Srinagar. It was during the drive that I realised the preciousness of time, the obstacles in the way like a traffic jam, the barricade blocking the road leading to the hospital. My friends were trying hard to remove it to save time.

Finally, I was there in the operation theatre. I made a conscious effort to tell the doctors whatever I could, I told them that to my knowledge I had received three bullet wounds. They asked me to move my limbs, which I did, I told them my name, my address, etc. I could hear them talking amongst themselves, they were saying that my condition was very critical and perhaps I would not survive for more than a few minutes. Hearing this, I became even more tense. I clearly remember asking them – will I survive? They said, yes I would. But what else could those doctors have told me at that time? I heard them planning how to cut the skull to explore the path of the bullet, which was a very scary thought, but they didn't do that finally. Instead, they plugged the wounds with gauze, which was very painful, even more painful than the bullets. A tracheotomy was also done – my throat was slit and I was kept on an artificial respiratory system. I had lost a lot of blood by that time. After the operation was completed, I lost my power of speech and swallowing. Another shock, but luckily I did not become unconscious at any point in time and neither did the doctors give me any anaesthesia, perhaps because I had sustained a head injury.

Thereafter, I shifted to the Medical Institute in Srinagar, where my friend Muzaffar who is a doctor was on duty that day. He helped me a great deal and was with me during all those trying moments when I was taken from one hospital to another in the ambulance for X-rays and MRIs. These tests revealed that the bullet had ripped through the brain and damaged its covering – some of the cranial nerves had been burnt, seared by the heat of the bullet.

For the next three days, the cerebrospinal fluid in which the brain floats, was leaking through my nose and mouth, the result of the damages caused to the nerves. My vocal chords were paralysed, tongue and palate were paralysed and there was a partial paralysis to the right side of my face, the upper eyelid of the right eye and the shoulder muscles. There were multiple fractures and grave muscle injuries. My recovery was long and painful, the damaged nerves never healed. I am told that nerves don't regenerate. I could not talk for many weeks together. My world was very quiet during those days with writing being the only means of communication. I was also not in a position to swallow anything and was living with the support of artificial systems. But I made an effort to put this behind me, and my friends and relatives were there to support me.

This is the most important experience of my life and it happened when I had just started my career in journalism. More than anything else, this experience taught me the importance of 'Safety in Journalism'. Indeed, no piece of journalism is more important than life and it's very important to be alert and use one's common sense every time.

Anyway, once I was healed, I got back into journalism with a conscious effort to focus on the positive aspects of life.

When I learnt that some Kashmiri youth were trying hard to get a break in the world of modelling and were ready to look beyond the circle of violence, it instantly caught my imagination. I thought the story was a very positive one. Another interesting factor was that the young aspirants from the Valley were giving modelling performances with the models from the Pandit community in a migrant camp of Kashmiri Pandits. They were all Kashmiris separated by circumstances.

All the models were teenagers born after the turmoil erupted in the Valley. They did not know of the poor living conditions of Kashmiri Pandits in the migrant camps of Jammu, and the Kashmiri Pandit children had not visited the Valley even once. That added another dimension to the story.

But I noticed that once the people of the two communities were face to face, the distances became irrelevant. It seemed that they had never been separated from one other, in fact, they were helping and passing on tips to each other.

After speaking to them, I gathered that the Kashmiri youth want to work towards a better future. The problem is that they don't receive proper guidance and direction. But this was a beginning and I was glad to be able to record it for the future.